# THE FACSIMILE TEXT SOCIETY

## SERIES V: ECONOMICS

---

VOLUME 2

JOHN WHEELER

A TREATISE OF COMMERCE

# JOHN WHEELER

# A TREATISE OF COMMERCE

Reproduced from the London Edition of 1601

## WITH A BIBLIOGRAPHICAL NOTE

### BY

### GEORGE BURTON HOTCHKISS

PUBLISHED FOR

# THE FACSIMILE TEXT SOCIETY

### BY

## COLUMBIA UNIVERSITY PRESS

### NEW YORK : M·CM·XXXI

Printed in the United States of America
by The National Process Company, New York

# BIBLIOGRAPHICAL NOTE

*A Treatise of Commerce* by John Wheeler was published in 1601, as a defense of the Society of Merchants Adventurers of England, which was then the strongest of the "regulated" trading companies. Two editions of the *Treatise* were printed; one in Middelburgh, Zeeland, the foreign headquarters of the company, the other in London. The present reprint is from a copy of the London edition in the Seligman Library of Columbia University.

The Middelburgh edition was doubtless the earlier by a few months. The author signed his dedication on June 6, 1601, at Middelburgh. A copy of the book was entered with the Stationers Company of London for printing there by John Harison on August fourteenth. That this was a printed copy of the Middelburgh edition seems evident from the fact that the entry in the Stationers' Register contains the same typographical error ("commodies" for "commodities") that appears on the title page of the Middelburgh edition. There are also indications that the format of the London edition was modeled upon that of the Middelburgh edition, although a smaller size of type was used.

Both editions are fine examples of printing, for their time. The Middelburgh edition is perhaps the handsomer of the two. Richard Schilders, the Dutchman who printed it, had worked as a journeyman in England before setting up his press in Middelburgh, and some of the most famous English books of the period bear his imprint. The larger size of type, of course, gave him an advantage. His edition contains 184 printed pages. Of these only 178 are numbered; the title-page and epistle dedicatory at the beginning and the page of *errata* at the end have no page numbers.

The London edition, printed by John Harison, has 126 pages, and the page numbering begins with the title page. The smaller type may not have been chosen simply for economy. The rules of the Stationers Company limited large-type editions to 1500 copies, whereas small-type editions might run to 3000. If more copies were desired, the type had to be reset and an entirely new edition printed. This meant waste of time as well as expense.

That the London edition was more numerous than the Middelburgh edition is suggested by the fact that more copies of it have survived. Only three copies of the Middelburgh edition are listed in the Short Title Catalog (by Pollard and Redgrave); of these, one is in the British Museum Library, one in the Harmsworth Library and one in the Henry E. Huntington Library. Seven specimens of the London edition are known; two in the British Museum Library, two in the Bodleian Library, one in the Cambridge University Library, one in the Henry E. Huntington Library, and one in the Seligman Library.

The variants in the two editions seem, at first glance, to be numerous, but upon closer study they resolve themselves almost entirely into mere variations in spelling, of no great significance. Nowhere are there clear evidences that the author made any revisions between the two printings. Possibly he did not even see the London edition through the press. He appends a list of "faultes escaped in printing" to the Middelburgh edition but no page of *errata* appears in the London edition, although the typographical errors in this also are quite frequent.*

Elizabethan spelling is notoriously variable and the variants in the two editions represent the practice of the two printers, Schilders and Harison. Harison is distinctly nearer to modern practice. This may be due to the fact that Schilders had gained his knowledge of English printing some twenty years earlier and perhaps had not kept closely in touch with the development of English orthography since that time. Harison, in the London edition, uses fewer doubled letters, fewer superfluous "e's" at the end of words and fewer capitals. He shows a tendency to replace the ending "ie" by "y." In the Middelburgh edition we find *twoo, fitt, woord, manie, rowe, witt,* and *withall;* the corresponding forms in the London edition are *two, fit, word, many, row, wit,* and *withal.* However, Harison is by no means consistent in this

---

*Two important *errata* should be noted: p. 57, l. 20, the word *not* is omitted from the phrase, "it sufficeth for al" (Middelburgh edition reads, "it suffiseth not for all"); p. 111, l. 31, the word *of* is inserted in the phrase, "Kind of usage" (Middelburgh edition reads, "Kinde usage." These are undoubtedly errors of the London printer.

practice. He shows merely a tendency toward simpler spelling, rather than a settled policy. Occasionally he drops a final "e" or undoubles a letter (e.g., *els* for *else*, *fal* for *fall*, *maner* for *manner*) where modern usage has retained the longer forms.

Both printers spell certain words in several different ways, sometimes on the same page, for no discoverable reason except caprice or the exigencies of spacing out a line. Both use the circumflex accent to indicate the omission of an "m" or "n" whenever it suits their convenience. This habit leads to some curious contrasts. For example on page 8 of the London edition the word *ordinances* appears twice; the second time it is spelt *ordinâces*. In the corresponding passage in the Middelburgh edition it first appears as *ordinâces* and then as *ordinances*.

The *Treatise of Commerce* is the only published work of John Wheeler. Little is known with certainty about him except that he was Secretary of the Merchants Adventurers and in 1608 compiled the Laws and Ordinances of the Company in permanent form. A ponderous manuscript volume containing his compilation, with additions by later hands, is one of the treasures of the British Museum. It was reprinted in 1902 by Dr. W. E. Lingelbach.*

This John Wheeler, Secretary of the Merchants Adventurers, was in all probability, John Wheeler, the Elder, of Great Yarmouth, who was born about

---

*"The Merchant Adventurers of England, their Laws and Ordinances," edited by W. E. Lingelbach (in the Series of Translations and Reprints issued by the Department of History, University of Pennsylvania) 1902.

1553, or slightly earlier, and who died about 1610. Shortly after the publication of the *Treatise of Commerce* he was elected to Parliament as one of the burgesses of the Port of Great Yarmouth and retained his seat until his death.

Wheeler's *Treatise of Commerce* has been extensively quoted by economic historians, but has never before been reprinted in its entirety. However, a carefully edited reprint of the Middelburgh edition with historical introduction by the writer of this bibliographical note was recently published by the New York University Press.

GEORGE BURTON HOTCHKISS

NEW YORK UNIVERSITY
May, 1931

# A
# TREATISE OF
## COMMERCE.

Wherein are shewed the Commodi-
*ties arising by a well ordered and ruled Trade, such
as that of the Societie of Merchants Aduenturers is proued to be :*

Written principally for the better information of
those who doubt of the Necessarinesse of
the said societie in the State of the
Realme of England.

*By* IOHN WHEELER, *Secretarie to
the said Societie.*

*Printed at London by Iohn
Harison.* 1601.

# To the Right Honourable Sir Ro-
### BERT CECILL *Knight, principall Secretary*
### to her Maieltie, &c.

*Hose which heretofore (Right Ho-
norable) haue written of anie matter, and had opinion, that the publishing thereof might doe good vnto
others, haue vsed to Dedicate their
Labours to some one, or other, vnder whose countenance, and protection the same might go foorth, &
bee the better lyked, and receyued of all men : which is the
cause that I haue made bolde to inscribe this Treatise,
such as it is, vnto your Honour, vpon hope of fauourable
allowance, and Patronage, which I instantlie craue, and
entreat, and withall, that in the readinge thereof, your
Honour would vouchsafe to remember, that it concerneth
those men, and that olde and ancientlie renoumed Companie of* MERCHANTES ADVENTVRERS,
*which was so well esteemed of, and highlie fauoured by your
late right Honorable Father, of woorthie memorie, vnto
whom as God hath appointed your Honour to be a Succes-
sour in manie excellent thinges of this life, whether wee
regarde the Honourable places, whereunto you are called in
the Gouernement of the State, or the vertues, and qualities
fit for so waightie a calling, wherewith you are endewed,
So it may please your Honour to take vnto you this Succes-*

*sion*

sion also, to witte, the dewtifull Observancie, and Promptitude, which the said Companie alwayes shewed towardes your said right Honourable Fathers seruice, and which they also stande readie and desirous to present, & performe vnto your Honour to their best power, and abilitie.

I am not ignorant also, that it is the maner of writers, to fill vp the greatest parte of their Prefaces with the praises, and comendations of those, to whome they Dedicate their Trauailes, and surelie this Reward seemeth to bee dew vnto true Vertue, that the Memorie thereof should bee consecrated to Posteritie, which can not be performed by anie Monument better, then by Bookes. And albeit, without all Glosinge, or counterfeyting, I haue heere in verie deed a large fielde of your Honours prayses offered vnto mee, yet because my simplicitie not onelie abhorreth all Adulation, but withall all kinde of Fawninge, or flattering speeche, and that your Honours singular Modestie, is wonte, not to abide anie thinge lesse, then euen the modestest commendations, I will let passe the same, and come vnto the handlinge of the ensuing Treatise, which with my selfe I humbly recommend vnto your Honcurs good fauour, and so beseech the Almightie to blesse, and keepe your Honour. Middelburgh the sixth of Iune 1601.

Your Honors with his seruice
at commandement.

IOHN WHEELER.

# A TREATISE OF
## COMMERCE.

Wherein are shewed the Commodities arising by
a well ordered and ruled Trade, such as that of the societie of MERCHANTS ADVENTVRERS
is prooued to be: Written for the better information
of those, who doubt of the necessarinesse of the
said Societie in the State of the Realme of
England, By *Iohn VVheeler*, Secretarie
to the saide Societie.

*Vita ciuilis in Societate est, Societas in Imperio, & Commercio.*

*Commercio gentes mari, montibúsque discreta miscentur,
vt quod vsquam nascitur, apud omnes affluat.*

Here be two points about the which the
Royal office & administration of a Prince is
wholy emploied, to wit, about the gouernment of the persons of men : next of things
conuenient and fit for the maintenance of
humane societie: wherin principally the ci-
uil life consisteth & hath her being: And therefore the Prince
that loueth the Policie, and ruleth by sage and good counsell,
is to constitute and appoint certaine Lawes, and ordinarie
Rules, both in the one and the other of the abouesaid points,
and specially in the first as the chiefest, which is conuer-
sant and occupied about the institution of the persons of men
in pietie, ciuill conuersation in maners and fashion of life, and
finally in the mutuall dutie of equitie & charitie one towards
another : of the which my purpose is not to intreat, but somewhat of that other point, namely, the Gouernment of things
conuenient and fit for the maintenance of Humane So-

cietie:

cietie: wherevnto mens actions and affections are chieflie
directed, and whereabouts they bestow, and employ not only the quickenes and industrie of their spirites, but also the labour and trauaile of their handes, and sides: that so they may
drawe from thence either commoditie or pleasure, or at least-
wise therby supplie, & furnish their seuerall wantes, and neces-
sities From hence, as from a root or fountain first proceedeth
the estate of *Marchandise*, and then consequentlie in a row,
so manie, diverse, and sundrie Artes, as we see in the worlde.
At which it should seeme that man beginneth the train, or
course of his life, and therein first of all discouereth not onlie
the dexteritie & sharpenes of his wit, but withal that naughti-
nes & corruption which is naturallie in him: for there is nothing in the world so ordinarie, and naturall vnto men, as to
contract, truck, merchandise, and traffike one with an other,
so that it is almost vnpossible for three persons to conuerse
together two houres, but they wil fal into talk of one bargaine
or another, chopping, changing, or some other kinde of contract Children, assoone as euer their tongues are at libertie,
doe season their sportes with some merchandise, or other: and
when they goe to schoole, nothing is so common among
them as to change, and rechange, buy and sell of that, which
they bring from home with them. The Prince with his subiects, the Maister with his seruants, one friend and acquain-
tance with another, the Captaine with his souldiers, the Husband with his wife, Women with and among themselues,
and in a word, all the world choppeth and changeth, runneth
& raueth after Marts, Markets and Merchandising, so that all
thinges come into Commerce, and passe into traffique (in
a maner) in all times, and in all places: not onely that, which
nature bringeth forth, as the fruits of the earth, the beasts, and
liuing creatures, with their spoiles, skinnes and cases, the met-
tals, minerals, and such like things, but further also, this man
maketh merchandise of the workes of his owne handes, this
man of another mans labour, one selleth words, another maketh taffike of the skins & bloud of other men, yea there are
some found so subtill and cunning merchants, that they per-
swade

ſwade and induce men to ſuffer themſelues to bee bought
and ſold, and we haue ſeene in our time enow, and too many
which haue made merchandiſe of mens ſoules. To conclude,
all that a man worketh with his hand, or diſcourſeth in his ſpi-
rit, is nothing els but merchandiſe, and a triall to put in practiſe the Contracts, which the Legiſts and men skilfull in the
lawes knew not to name otherwiſe then thus, *Do vt des, Fa-
cio vt facias* : the which words in effect comprehend in them
all negotiations, or traffiques whatſoeuer, and are none o-
ther thing but meere matter of merchandiſe & Commerce.
Now albeit this affection bee in all perſons generally both
high and low, yet there are of the notableſt, and principalleſt
Traffiquers which are aſhamed, and thinke ſcorne to be cal- *Commendation*
led Merchants : whereas indeed merchandiſe, which is vſed *of Merchandiſe.*
by way of proper vacation, being rightly conſidered of, is
not to be deſpiſed, or accounted baſe by men of iudgement,
but to the contrarie, by many reaſons and examples it is to be
proued, that the eſtate is honorable, & may be exerciſed not
only of thoſe of the third eſtate (as we terme thē) but alſo by
the Nobles, and chiefeſt men of this Realme with commendable profit, and without any derogation to their Nobilities,
high Degrees, and conditions, with what great good to their
ſtates, honour, and enriching of themſelues and their Countries, the *Venetians, Florentines, Genoueſes*, and our neighbours
the *Hollanders* haue vſed this trade of life, who knoweth not ?
or hauing ſeene the beautie, ſtrength, opulencie, and popu-
louſneſſe of the abeueſaid Cities and prouinces, wondereth
not thereat? Was not this the firſt ſtep, and entrie of the kings
of Portugall vnto the kingdomes and riches of the Eaſt? *Solon*
in his youth gaue himſelfe to the feate of Merchandiſe, and in
his time, ſaith *Plutarch* (bringing *Heſiodus* for his author) there *Plutarch. in vita*
was no eſtate of life reprochful, neither Art, or occupatiō, that *Solonis.*
did put difference betweene men, but rather which is more,
merchādiſe was accoūted an honorable thing, as that which
miniſtred the meanes to haunt and traffique with barbarous
nations, to procure the friendſhip of Princes, and to gaine experience into many matters, in ſo much (ſaith he) that there
haue

haue been Merchants, which were founders of great Cities, as
he was that founded *Merseilles* in France. The wise *Thales
Milesins* did also exercise Merchandise : likewise *Hippocrates*
and *Plato* defrayed the charges of a voyage, which hee made
in *Egypt*, with the monie which he got there by selling of oile:
So that it appeareth, that not only a Prince may vse this kinde
of men, I meane Merchantes, to the great benefite, and good
of his state, either for forreigne intelligence, or exploration,
or for the opening of an entrie & passage vnto vnknowne and
faire distant partes, or for the furnishing of monie, and other
provisions in time of warres, and dearth, or lastly, for the ser-
vice and honor of the Prince, and Coũtrie abroad at all times
requisite, and expedient, but also this kinde of life may be ex-
ercised and vsed with commendation, and without losse of on
jote of honor in those, who are honorable, or of eminent de-
gree, as aforesaid : Wherevnto I adde this further, that without Merchandise, no ease or commodious liuing continueth
long in anie state, or common wealth, no not loyaltie, or e-
quitie it selfe, or vpright dealing. Therefore herein also, as in
the former point, good order and rule is to be set, where it is
wanting, or where it is alreadie established, there it ought to
be preserued: for the maintenance of so necessarie, and beneficiall an estate in the common Wealth, by constituting meet
& well proportioned ordinances ouer the same, & ouer those
things, which are thereupon depending, between the Marchants, and those things, which are marchandized, or handled likewise with convenable, and well appropriated Magi-
strates and ouerseers for the maintenance, & execution of the
said ordináces. For it is very certain & true, that *sine imperio nec
domus vlla, nec Ciuitas, nec Gens, nec societas, nec hominũ vniuersum genus stare, nec rerũ natura omnis, nec misdus ipse potest, &c.*

The peaceable, politike, and rich Prince King *Henrie 7.*
well marking the trueth hereof, and perceiuing that as in former times, so in his manie disturbances, grievances and damages had befallen to, and among the English M. M. his subiects, trading into the low countries, *ob defectũ boni Regiminis*,
tooke order for the same, as well by cõfirming the ancient
Charters

Charters of his Predeceſſors, Kings of England vnto the Societie of M. M. Aduenturers, as alſo by adding thereunto
newe, whereby hee ſo ſtrengthened, and enlarged the authoritie, and Priuiledges of the ſaid Fellowſhip, that euer
ſince the ſame hath floriſhed in great proſperitie, and wealth,
and out of it (as out of a plentifull Nurſerie, haue ſprung
and proceeded almoſt all the principall Marchants of this
Realme, at the leaſt ſuch Companies, as haue ariſen ſince,
haue for the moſt part, fetched their light, patterne, and forme
of policie and trade from the ſaid Societie to the ineſtimable
good and commoditie of this Realme, our natiue Countrey:
ſo that to change this courſe were to returne to the olde con-
fuſion, and diſorder, and withall to bereaue the land of ſo ne-
ceſſarie and ſeruiceable an eſtate, as *Merchandiſe is.*

Whatſoeuer is commendable, or is ſaid of the beſt founded Companie or Merchantes in generall, maketh alſo for
the Companie of Marchants Aduenturers ſpecially: howbeit theſe things are particularly for our purpoſe to be conſidered in this Companie: *The firſt Inſtitution: The Auncient eſti-*
*mation it hath had: The ſtate and Gouernment of it, and ſuch be-*
*nefits, as grow to the Realme by the maintenance of it.*

---

*Of the firſt Inſtitution of the Fellowſhip or Companie of*
*Merchants Aduenturers, and the cauſes thereof.*

ARCVS *Cato*, a prudent Coun-
ſellour, and a good husband in deed,
ſaith: *Quòd oportet Patremfamilias ven-*
*da em eſſe non emacem:* And who knoweth not, that we haue no ſmall need of
many things, whereof foreigne Countreys haue great ſtore, and that wee may
well ſpare many things, whereof the ſaid
Countreys haue alſo need? Now to vent the ſuperfluities of
our Countrey, and bring in the Commodities of others, there
is no readier, or better meane then by Merchandize: and

B                         ſeeing

seeing we haue no way to encreaſe our treaſure by mynes
of golde and ſiluer at home, and can haue nothing from a-
broad without mony, or ware, it followeth neceſſarily, that
the aboueſaid good counſel of *Cato*, to be ſellers and not buyers, is to be followed, yet ſo, that wee carry not out more in
value ouer the ſeas then we bring home ſrō thence, or tranſ-
port things hurtfull to the State, for this were no good huſ-
bandry, but tendeth to the ſubuerſion of the land and dimini-
ſhing of the treaſure thereof, whereas by the other wee ſhall
greatly encreaſe it, the trade being carried and managed vnder a conuenient gouernment & orders, and not in a diſper-
ſed, looſe, and ſtragling maner: the practiſe whereof we may
ſee in this Realme almoſt theſe 400. yeeres together: Firſt
in the Staple, and Wooll trade, and next in that of the Merchants Aduenturers and Cloth trade. And King *Edward* the
third thought it not enough, to bring the working and making of the Cloth into the realme, except, when the ſame was
indraped, he withal prouided for the vent thereof in forreigne

parts, to the moſt benefit and aduancement of that newe begun Arte, and therefore whereas the aboueſaid Company
(though then otherwiſe termed thē now) in the yeere 1248.
had obtained Priuiledges of *Iohn* Duke of *Brabant*, the ſaid
King confirmed the ſame for the ſubſtantiall gouernment of
the ſaid Company in their trade.

In the yeere 1399. The Arte of making of Cloth being
growen to good perfection within this Realme, King *Henrie*
the Fourth firſt prohibited the inuection of forreigne made
Cloth, and gaue vnto the ſaid Company a very beneficiall
and ample Charter of Priuiledges, confirmed by Acte of
Parliament for the ſame purpoſe and intent, as his Predeceſ-
ſor King *Edward* the Third had done before him: whoſe example the ſucceeding Kings, *Henrie* the fifth, and ſixt, *Edward* the fourth, and *Richard* the third followed, ratifying and
confirming their Predeceſſors doings on this behalſe: the
next in order following King *Henrie* the ſeauenth, like a wiſe
and prouident Prince, well marking and conſidering howe
neceſſary and ſeruiceable the ſtate of *Merchandiſe* was vnto
this

this Realme, not onely liked and confirmed that, which the a-
boue rehearfed Kings had done before him, but alfo greatly
enlarged and augmented the fame by three feuerall Charters, and by other his gracious and royall faucurs from time
to time, not onely towards the faid Company in generall, but
withall to diuers Merchants in particular: *Mercatores ille fæ-* Polidorus in vi-
*penumero pecuniæ multa data gratuito iuuabat, vt Mercatura* ta Henrici fep-
*(Ars vnæ omnium cunctis æque mortalibus tum commoda, tum* timi.
*neceffaria)in fuo Regno copiofior effet.* And when vpon a vari-
ance fallen out betweene him & the Archduke *Philip*, he had
drawen as well the faid Company as that of the Staple out of
the low Countries, and placed them at *Calice*, hee gaue vnto
them within the faid Towne as large and beneficiall Priuiledges, as they before had enioyed in the faid lowe Countries,
which were very large and fauourable, intituling them by the
name of *Merchants Aduenturers.* And albeit in this Kings
dayes, as alfo in the raigne of King *Henrie* the fourth, the like
complaint as of late, was made by the Clothiers, Wooll-
growers, Dyers, &c. againft the Company of Merchants Aduenturers: yet after due examination of the faid complaint,
the iffue procured great fauour to the faid Company, & gaue
occafió of the inlarging of their former Charters, with an expreffe reftraint of all Straglers, and Entermedlers, that might
difturbe, or impeach their trade : and whereas alfo the *Eafter-*
*lings* at this time had entered into the fame trade, the aforefaid prudent Prince King *Henrie* the feuenth, did not onely
ftraightly inhibite them fo to doe, but alfo tooke Recogni-
zance of twenty thoufand Markes of the Aldermen of the
Steelyarde at *London*, that the faid *Eafterlings* fhould not cary
any Englifh cloth to the place of Refidence of the Merchants
Aduenturers in the lowe Countries, or open their Fardels of
Cloth in the faid Countries, to the preiudice of the faid Company, by putting the fame to vent there, which they were not
wont to do. In the time of the reigne of K. *E.* the *6. Iohn Tulle*,
*Iohn Dimock* & others, brethrē of the faid Cópany, enformed
the Bifhop of Elye, at that time L. Châcellor, of matter againft
the Cópany, but their bil brought to the Councel boord, and

exami-

examined, it was finally ordered, that the said Complainants
should submit themselues vnto the obedience of the Companies orders, and pay certaine fines, which the Lordes then
laid vpon them, besides that two of the principallest found to
be the Ringleaders of the rest, were committed to the Fleet,
there to remaine, till such time as the Company of M M. Aduenturers should sue for their release. And albeit the said
persons renewed their complaints, in the first yeere of Q.
*Maries* raigne, and did put vp a bill to the Parliament house,
against the Company, yet the same being answered by the
said Company, was reiected, and cast out of the Parliament
house. Since the time of King *Henrie* the seuenth, the succeeding Princes, King *Henrie* the eight of famous memorie,
King *Edward* the sixth, and Queene *Marie*, haue continued,
confirmed, and enlarged the abouesaid Charters and
Priuiledges, but aboue all other, our most gracious Soueraigne, that now raigneth, Queene ELIZABETH, hath
shewed her gracious, and fauourable affection towardes the
said Companie, in not onely confirming the letters Patentes,
and Charters of her most Noble Grandfather, and of other
her Highnesse Predecessours aboue mentioned, but also in
adding thereunto other more large, and beneficiall Priuiledges of her owne. For whereas the M.M. Aduenturers about
the beginning of her Maiesties reigne, by diuerse restraints,
Edicts, and Proclamations, made and set forth by the Gouernours and Commanders of the Low Countryes, were em-
peached and prohibited to trade into the said Countries, contrarie to the ancient Entercourses, and the Priuiledges to the
said Company granted of old time, & consequently were oc-
casioned to seeke, and erect a Trade in the partes of Germanie, which they did with their great charges and trauaile for
the vent of the Commodities of the Realme, her Highnes calling to remembrance this and other faithfull & acceptable seruice at sundrie times done by the sayd M.M. Aduenturers in
diuerse the great & waighty affaires of her Maiesty & realme,
and minding the encrease and aduancement of the said Merchants, as much as any her Progenitours, (as her Highnesse
profes-

professeth in the said Charter) it pleased her said Maiestie in the sixt yere of her reigne, to giue and grant vnto them those gracious and ample priuiledges, which the said Companie now enioyeth, and afterwards vpon new occasion, the trade of the said Company being much impeached by wrongfull entermedling of vnfree persons in the same, it pleased her Maiestie by a new Charter, and Letters Patents vnder the great, seale of England, in the eight & twentith yeare of her reigne, to prouide against such iniurious, and vnorderly intrusion, acknowledging the seruices done to her Highnesse by the said M. M. Aduenturers, and pronouncing them to haue beene, & to be verie beneficiall members to the generall state of the realme and common wealth of England: which notable testimonie of so incomparable a Princesse after so many yeares of experience and triall, may alone, if there were none other, serue for a full & sufficient Apologie of the abouesaid Company of M. M. Aduenturers, against all the priuie & open, forreigne, and domestical gaine-saiers, slanderers, & oppugners of the same, and withall, for a certaine and infallible argumēt, that for the vent of wooll, and woollen wares (the principall commodities of the Realme) it is most profitable both for the Prince and countrie, to vse a gouerned Companie, and not to permit a promiscuous, stragling, and dispersed trade, whereof I shall haue occasion to say more, when I come to shew the benefices, which do arise vnto the Common-wealth of England, by the maintenance of the abouesaid Companie, & the gouernment therein vsed.

---

*Of the ancient estimation which the Company of*
*Merchants aduenturers hath had.*

 Y that which hath bene aboue said of the Institution of the Fellowship or company of M. M. Aduēturers, is partly shewed in what estimation the said Companie hath been hitherto with the Kings and Queenes of this realme, from

the

the reigne of King *Edward* the third, a sufficient motiue and reason, as may be well thought for the present and future a-ges, to haue the said Compauie in no lesse estimation and li-king : but this is not all, for if we would but looke out of En-gland to our neighbors in Germany and the low Countries, we should see the Merchants Aduenturers manie ages toge-ther sought for, welcomed, embraced, cherished, and vsed in as good, yea oftentimes in better tearmes, then the Naturals of the said Countries themselues, as appeareth by the ancient Charters, large and beneficiall Priuiledges, and exemptions granted to the said Companie by sundry Princes, States, Ci-ties, and Commonwealths of high and low Dutchland, since the yeare of our Lord 1296. to this our time : which are yet extant to be shewed, to the great honour and benefite of this our natiue Countrie, & the Princes thereof from time to time: For thereby we haue not onely opened a passage and entrie into forreigne States and Countries, but also by our gainfull and beneficiall trade, haue made them the faster friends to the State of the Realme of England, and the English Nation; besides the great wealth and commoditie which hath arisen thereby to the Common-wealth.

After the taking of Calice by King *Edward* the third, the Earles and people of Flaunders, for the better assurance and safetie of their State, procured a league and entercourse with the Kings of England, and their Merchants: whereby the said Earles and people found in short time such profite and com-moditie, that *Lewes* Earle of Flaunders in the yeare 1358. gaue and granted to the English Merchants so large and am-ple Priuiledges and freedomes, that no Nation in Europe had the like in that Countrie at that time, by reason whereof, and that the aduenture by sea and land into Flaunders was very short & easie, & almost without danger, the Company setled themselues in the Towne of *Bridges*, & stapled their commo-dities there : which once knowne and blowne abroad, Mer-chants out of all parts of Europe resorted thither, and made their habitation there, which appeareth by the houses at this day stâding, which beare the names of the cities & countries, whence

*Companie of Merchants Ad-uenturers at Bridges.*

whence the said Strangers were. So that in few yeares all the
Townes in Flanders, especially *Bridges*, were growne to such
wealth and prosperitie, that the same thereof went almost
through the whole earth; and at this day, although their
great opulencie and concourse of Merchants be altogether
failed, yet in many Countries of Christendome, and out of
Christendome, all the Netherlanders carie the name of Flemings, and the low Countries of Flanders. After this, when
the Flemings through wealth and fulnesse of bread, did for-
get their bounden dutie to their Prince, and withall grew to
a proud disdaine and contempt of all Merchants strangers,
and in particular of the English, by whom they had receiued
their chiefest good and welfare, the Company remoued from
*Bridges* to a Towne in Zeland called Middelbourgh, where
they are now at this present residing, whither all other Nations followed the straight. Since which, those of Bridges fee-
ling the smart of their folly, haue many times made sute and
meanes to draw the English thither againe, and in mans memorie they profered a great summe of money vnto the said
Merchants, with offer of more ample Priuiledges and immunities, then euer they had before in Bridges, or any where els;
yea in a maner they profered a blancke, to tie them to what
the English thought good, to haue the traffike againe in their
Towne, which very fondly when they had it they could not
keepe. This Towne of Middelbourgh stood so neere the sea,
that the ditches & low places round about, being continually
full of salt and filthy oaze, for want of a fresh Riuer or current
to cleanse the same, bred such stench and noysome sauours,
that the English vsed to a wholesome and sweete aire in their
owne country, were troubled with grieuous Agues, and other
sore diseases, & for their health sake, were forced to leaue the
said towne, about the yeare of our Lord 1444. At which time
Antwerp being but a poore and simple Towne, standing in
Brabant, made great sute to the Companie to repaire thither,
which they finally vpon offer of verie large and beneficiall
Priuiledges, obtained. In which towne of Antwerp, and the
town of *Bergen op Zoom* likewise in Brabat, the Copany euer
since hath for the most part cotinued, saue that (as aforesaid) in

*Companie of Merchants Aduenturers leaue Bridges, and repaire to Middelburgh.*

the time of king *Henrie* the seuenth, they were vpon occasion
remoued to Calice for a time, till that by the earnest intercession of the Lady *Margaret* Duchesse of Sauoy, they repaired
againe into the Low Countries, first to Middelburgh, then
afterwards to Antwerp, where they were ioyfully and honorably receiued, and entertained by the Magistrate and chiefest citizens of the Towne, comming forth in solemne procession to meete and welcome the said Merchants, as by the
Records of those times sufficiently appeareth. And heere by

*Estate of Antwerp at the Companies first comming thither.*
the way, it is not much from our purpose, to insert somewhat
of the state of Antwerp, at the first comming thither of the
Companie, wherin a man shall see that which is almost incredible: *Philip* surnamed the *Good*, Duke of Burgundie, and of
Brabant, &c. gaue Priuiledges to the Companie, vnder the
name of the English Nation, by which name the said Company euer since hath beene most commonly knowne in the
low Countries, which happened in the yeare 1446. Which
Priuiledges the towne of Antwerp confirmed the sixt of August in the abouesaid yeare, giuing to them besides a large
house, which is now called the old *Burse*, and afterwards by
exchāge, another more goodly, spacious & sumptuous house
called the *Court of Lier* which the Companie enioyed till the
said town was yeelded vp to the Duke of Parma, in the yeare
1585. At the abouesaid first Concordate, and conclusion of
Priuiledges with the towne of Antwerp, or not long before,
there were not in all the Towne aboue foure Merchants, and
those also no aduenturers to the sea, the rest of the Inhabitāts
or Townsmen were but meane people, and neither able, nor
skilfull to vse the feat or trade of Merchandise, but did let out
the best of their houses to English-men, and other strangers
for chambers, and pack-houses, contenting themselues with
some corner for their profits sake : but within few yeares the
concourse, and resort of forreigne Merchants to that Towne
was so great, that house roome waxed scant, rents were raised, Tolles, axcises, & all other duties to the Prince & Towne
wonderfully encreased, and the Antwerp men themselues,
who in few yeares before were but meane artificers, or liued

by

by husbandrie, and keeping of cattell (whereof one gate of that citie to this day beareth the name) and had but sixe ships belonging to their Towne, and those for the Riuer onely, *De Coe Poort.* that neuer went to sea, began to grow exceeding rich, so that some fell to the trade of Merchandise, and others employed their substance in building, the their old rotten houses couered with thatch, were pulled downe, their waste ground, whereof there was store within the Towne, was turned into goodly buildings. and faire streetes, & their shipping encreated accordingly: thus prospered not only those of Antwerp, but all other Townes and places thereabouts, so that in our memorie that now liue, the said Towne was growne to such wealth, strength & beautie, as neuer none the like in so short a time, and no maruel, for within the compasse of fistie yeeres an house that was worth but fourtie Dallers a yeare, grewe to be worth three hundred Dallers a yeere, and an house that was let out for sixtie Dallers, came afterwards to be let for *A Daller is three* foure hundred Dallers, yea some houses in Antwerpe were *shillings sterling.* let for 600. some for 800. Dallers a yeare rent: besides their Hauens for ships to come and lade and discharge within the Towne: their publike stately buildings, and edifices, erected partly for ornament, and partly for the ease and accommodating of the Merchant, were so costly and sumptuous, as he that hath not seene and marked them well, would not beleeue it: to say nothing of the fortification of the Towne, which is such, that the charges thereof would trouble the richest Prince in Eurorpe: but as the Poet *Lucan* said,

*Inuida Fatorum series summisq, negatum stare diu.*

So it fareth at this day with Antwerp, for it hath within these few yeares suffered verie great change and alteration, and more is like to do, if it long continue shut vp, & without trade and traffike, vnder the yoke of the Spaniard, and the feare of an impregnable castle stuffed with souldiers, a scourge and plague to that, and to all free Cities. Thus much by the way, of Antwerp, the late Packe-house of Europe, and of the state therof, when the English Merchants first repaired vnto it, and of the great wealth it grew vnto in verie short time, whereof

C     the

the faid Englifh Merchants with their gainfull and beneficiall trade were a great caufe, and meanes, which principally
made them to be fo much regarded and efteemed in the faid
Towne, and by the Princes and Gouernours thereof from
time to time, as well appeareth, among other proofes, by this

*Sleidanus 22. li-
bro Commenta-
riorum.*

one recorded by *Sleidan,* and remembred by fome that yet
liue. The Emperour *Charles* the fift would haue brought the
Inquifition into the Towne of Antwerp, in the yeare 1550.
whereabouts there was much ado, and great queftion, and
neither by the fute of the Towne, nor by any interceffion,
or requeft of their friends, could the faid Emperour be diuer-
ted from his purpofe: at the laft it was fhewed him, that if the

*Inquifition in
Antwerp left off
for the M. M.
Aduenturers
fake.*

Inquifition were brought in, he wold driue the Englifh Merchants out of that Citie, and out of the whole low Countries
alfo, the confequence whereof when he had wel confidered,
he changed his mind, and fo the Citie of Antwerp was faued
from the Inquifition, which they fo much feared, and by no
fute or meanes befides were able to put from them; of fuch
eftimation and account were the Merchants Aduenturers
with that mightie and prudent Emperour, and of fuch credit
and reckoning haue they beene from time to time at home
with eleuen Kings and Queenes of this Realme of England,
and abroad with the Cities of *Bridges* in Flanders, *Antwerpe,*
and *Bergen op den zoom* in Brabant, *Middelbourgh* and *Zie-
riczee* in Zeland, *Amfterdam* and *Dort* in Holland, *Vtrecht*
the chiefe Citie of a Prouince of that name, & with the Dukes
Earles, Lords, and Rulers of the abouefaid Cities & Prouinces, lying within the low Countries, ancient friends and confederates with the Crowne of England. And in Germanie
with the Townes of *Hambrough* and *Stade,* and the Earles of
*Eaft-friefland* fince the yeare 1564. till this day, at which
time they obtained Priuiledges of the Lady *Anne* Counteffe
of *Oldenburgh,* and her fonnes *Edgard* and *iohn,* wherein they
call the Company of Merchants Aduenturers, *Inclytam illam
& celebratam paffim Anglicorum Mercatorum Societatem.* In
all which places and countries the forefaid Company haue fo
demeaned themfelues, that thereby they haue reaped great
loue,

loue, credite, fame, and commendation, and haue left behind them a longing for them againe in thofe places, where they once refided or held their Marts, & procured a defire of them in many places, where they neuer were : which appeareth by the honourable teftimonie giuen of the Company by the a-bouefaid Townes, and forreigne princes abroad, and is other-wife well knowneto thofe, who know any thing of the do-ings of our Neighbours. And lately, when through the mali-cious and iniurious working of a few of the *Hanfe* Townes, in-ftigated & holpen forward by the King of Spaines minifters, a part of the faid Company was put from the Towne of *Stade* in the yeare 1597. and were forced to retire out of the Em-pire, the Townes of the vnited low Countreys, eleuen or twelue in number of the beft fituate, each ftriuing to be pre-ferred, like fo many Riuals or Competitors, offered theſelues in moft friendly and heartie fort, and inuited the faid Compa-nie to refide with them, vpon promifes of fuch fauour and pri-uiledge as ought neuer to be forgotten : but hereof poffibly enough. Let vs now looke into the Eftate, Policie, and go-uernement of the faid Companie, whereby we fhall plaine-ly fee the caufes and reafons of the loue, eftimation, and cre-dite which it hath purchafed abroad, and fo the fooner be-leeue that, which hath aboue beene fet downe, and affirmed.

*Of the State and Gouernement of the Companie of Merchants Aduenturers, and of fuch benefites as growe to the Realme by the maintenance there-of.*

He Company of the Merchants Aduen-turers confifteth of a great number of wealthie, and well experimented Mer-chants, dwelling in diuerfe great Cities, Maritime Townes, and other parts of the Realme, to wit, London, Yorke, Norwich,

Exceſter,

Exceter, Ipſwitch, Newcaſtle, Hull, &c. Theſe men of olde
time linked and bound themſelues together in Companie for
the exerciſe of Merchandiſe and ſea-fare, trading in Cloth,
Kerſie, and all other, as well Engliſh as forreigne Commodities vendible abroad, by the which they brought vnto the
places where they traded, much wealth, benefite, and commoditie, and for that cauſe haue obtained many verie excellent and ſingular priuiledges, rights, iuriſdictions, exemptions
and immunities, all which thoſe of the aforeſaid Fellowſhip
equally enioy after a well ordered maner and forme, and according to the ordinances, lawes, and cuſtomes deuiſed and
agreed vpon by common conſent of all the Merchants, free
of the ſaid Fellowſhip, dwelling in the abouenamed Townes
and places of the land : the parts and places which they trade
vnto, are the Townes and ports lying betweene the ſiuers of
*Somme* in France, and the *Scawe* in the Germane ſea: not into all at once, or at each mans pleaſure, but into one, or two
Towns at the moſt within the aboueſaid bounds, which they
commonly call the Mart Towne, or Townes ; for that there
onely they ſtapled the commodities, which they brought out
of England, & put the ſame to ſale, and bought ſuch forreigne
commodities, as the land wanted, and were brought from far
by Merchants of diuerſe Nations and countries flocking thither, as to a Faire, or market to buy & ſell. And albeit through
the troubles and alteration of times, the Merchants Aduenturers haue beene forced to change and leaue their olde
marte Townes, and ſeeke new (as hath beene partly touched
before) yet whereſoeuer they ſeated themſelues, thither presently repaired other Strangers, leauing likewiſe the places
whence the Engliſh Merchants were departed, and planting
themſelues where they reſided: ſo that as long as the Company continued their Mart, or Staple in a place, ſo long grew
and proſpered that place; but when they forſooke it, the welfare and good eſtate thereof ſeemed withall to depart, and
forſake it, as in olde time hath beene ſeene in *Bridges*, and in
our time in ſome others, and no maruell: for diligent inquiry
being made in the yeare 1550. by the comandement of the
Empe-

*The Companie
of M. Aduen-
turers is able to
make and diuert
a trade.*

Emperour *Charles* the fifth, what benefite or commoditie
came to his state of the low Countries, by the haunt and commerce of English Merchants: it was found, that in the Citie
of Antwerp alone, where the Compaine of Merchants Aduenturers was at time residing, were at least twenty thousand
persons fed and maintained for the most part by the trade
of the Merchants Aduenturers : besides thirtie thousand o-
thers in other places of the low Countries likewise maintained and fed partly by the said trade; partly by endraping of
cloth, and working in wool, and other commodities brought
out of England. In confirmation whereof, I haue heard ancient Merchants say, That at the time when the aboutsaid
Companie was entirely resident at Antwerpe, a little before
the troubles which fell out in the yeares 63. and 64. there
were fed and maintained in the low Countries sixtie thousand soules (and some haue said a great manie more) by the
English trade, and by the wares bought in the low countries
to be caried into England, which no doubt was the cause, that
the Princes of the low Countries haue beene so fauourable
to the abouesaid Companie, and so loth to forgoe or loose
them, as knowing that therewithall they should loose a verie
faire flower of their garland, yea a sure roote and foundation
of their wealth. For on the one side, such is the value, profite,
and goodnesse of the English commodities, that all Nations
of these parts of Europe, and elsewhere, desire them : and on
the other side, the English Merchants buy vp, and carrie into
England so great a quantitie of forreigne wares, that for the
sale thereof all strange Merchants do, and will repaire vnto *The profites ari-*
them. Now what these English commodities are, & how they *sing by the Mar-*
be so profitable, may appeare by the particulars following. *chants Aduen-*
*turers trade and*
First, there is shipped out yearely by the abouesaid Com- *residence beyond*
panie, at least sixtie thousand white Clothes, besides coloured *the seas.*
Clothes of all sorts, Kersies short, and long, Bayes, Cottons,
Northern Dosens, and diuerse other kinds of course Clothes.
The iust value of these sixtie thousand white Clothes cannot
well be calculated, or set downe, but they are not lesse worth
(in mine opinion) then sixe hundred thousand pounds ster-

ling, or Englifh mony. The coloured Clothes of all fortes,
Bayes, Kerfyes, Northern Dofens, and other courfe Clothes,
I reckon to arife to the number of fortie thoufand Clothes, at
leaft, and they bee woorth one with another foure hundred
thoufand poundes fterling, or Englifh mony.

There goeth alfo out of England, befides thefe Woollen
Clothes, into the low Countries, Wooll, Fel, Lead, Tinne, Saf-
forn, Conyskins, Leather, Tallow, Alablafter ftone, Corne,
Beef, and diuers other things, amounting vnto great fummes
of money: By al which Commodities, a number of labouring
men are fet on worke, and gaine much money, befides that
which the Merchants gaineth, which is no fmall matter. Herevnto adde the money which Shippers, and men that liue vpon the water, get by fraight and portage of the aforefaid
Commodities from place to place, which would amount to a
great fumme, if the particulars thereof were, or could be ex-
actly gathered: hereby in fhort may be feene, how great and
profitable the Company of the Merchants Aduenturers trade
hath beene, and is in the places where they hold their Refidence, befides the profit raifed vpon the Chambers, Sellers,
and Packhoufes, which they muft haue for foure or fiue hundred Merchants, whereby rents are maintained and kept vp,
and the great expenfes otherwife, which the faid Merchants
are at for their diet, apparell, &c. to fay nothing of the Princes, or Generalities profit, and reuenues by their Tolles, Con-
voyes, Impofts, Axcyfes, and other dueties, whereof there can
be no certaine notice had, but to fhew the greatnes thereof,
let this one figne fo long agoe ferue for all, that *Philip* the
*Good*, Duke of *Burgunds*, and firft founder of the order of the
*Golden Fleece*, gaue the aforefaid Fleefe for a liuerie or badge
of the faid Order, for that hee had his chiefeft Tolles, Reuenues, and Incoms, by Wooll and Woollen Cloth: Thus you
haue feene what profit is raifed by ftragers, vpon the Englifh
trade, it followeth to fhew, what the M. M. Aduenturers buy
for returne, of ftrange nations, and people frequenting their
Marte townes, & bringing their coutrey comodities thether.
Of the Dutche and Germane Merchants, they buy Rhe-
nifh

*Carion Libro. 5.*

*Germane wares.*

niſh Wine, Fuſtians, Copper, Steele, Hempe, Oinion ſeed, Copper and Iron Wyre, Latten, Kettles, and Pannes Linnen cloth, Harnas, Saltpeter, Gun-powder, all things made at *Norenbergh*, and in ſumme, there is no kinde of ware that Germanie yeeldeth, but generally the M. M. Aduenturers buye as much, or more thereof then any other nation.

Of the Italians, they buy all kinde of ſilke wares, Veluets, *Italian wares.* wrought and vnwrought, Taffitaes, Sattins, Damaskes, Sarſenets, Milan Fuſtians, Cloth of Gold and Siluer, Grograines, Chamlets. Sattin, and ſowing ſilke, Organzine, Orſoy, and all other kindes of wares either made or to be had in Italie.

Of the *Eaſterlings* they buye Flaxe, Hempe, Wax, Pitch, *Eaſterlings* Tarre, Wainſcot, Deal-bourds, Oares, Corne, Furres, Cables, *wares.* and Cable yearne, Tallow, Ropes, Maſtes for Shippes, Sopeaſhes, Eſtrigd wooll & almoſt whatſoeuer is made, or groweth in the Eaſt Countries.

Of the *Portingales* they buye all kinde of Spices and *Portingal wares.* Drugges: with the Spaniſh and French, they had not much to doe, by reaſon that our Engliſh Merchantes haue had a great trade in France and Spaine, & ſo ſerue England directly from thence with the Commodities of thoſe Countries.

Of the low Country Merchants, or Netherlanders, they *Netherlandiſh* buye all kinde of manufacture, or hand worke not made in *wares.* England, Tapeſtrie, Buckrams, White threed, Incle, Linnen cloth of all ſorts, Cambricks, Lawnes, Mather, and an infinite nūber of other things, too long to rehearſe in particular, but hereby I hope it ſufficiently appeareth, that it is of an exceeding valew, which the M. M. Aduenturers buye, and carry into England, in ſo much that I haue heard it credibly reported, that all the Commodities that come out of all other Countreys beſides England, were not wont to ſet ſo many people on worke in the low Countreys, as the Commodities which came out of England onely did, neither that any other two of the greateſt Nations that frequented the ſaid low Countries for trade, did buy, or cary out ſo much goods in value, as the M. M. Aduéturers: The knowledge, & cóſideration whereof hath made the thought worthy to be made of, cheriſhed,

rished, and defired by Princes, States, and Commonwealths, and it would not hurt the ftate of the Empire a whit, to hold friendfhip, and entertaine fo profitable a Companie & Trade as this, wherby great multitudes of their poore people might be fet on worke, and get their liuing, and in proceffe of time grow rich thereby as the men of Antwerp, and others of the low countries haue done, which by the practifes of the Pope and King of Spaine, and the vnreafonable dealing of the *Hanfes,* is in a maner kept from them. The root and fpring of all this almoſt incredible Trade and Traffique, hath had his increafe and proceeding from the politike gouernement, lawes, and orders deuifed, and obferued of olde time in the faid Companie, as aforefaid: efpecially fince the reigne of King *Henrie* the feuenth, by the fpeciall order, commandement, and encouragement of the faid noble Prince, one day ſtill being a Schoole-mafter vnto the other, and men by experience, vfe and knowledge of forreigne people, and their fafhions, orders, and kind of dealing, growing dayly and from time to time to an exacter courfe and greater perfection of matters, and vnderſtanding of their owne eſtate, and what is fitteſt for the vpholding, and maintenance therof: Thefe faid ordinances containe in them all kind of good difcipline, inſtruction and rules to bring vp youth in, and to keep them in order: fo that the Merchants Aduenturers dwelling in the aboue mentioned Cities and Townes of the Realme of England, fend their yong men, fonnes, and feruants, or Apprentifes, who for the moſt part are Gentlemens fonnes, or mens children of good means or qualitie, to the Mart Townes beyond the feas, there to learne good fafhions, and to gaine experience and knowledge in trade, and the maners of ſtrange Nations, thereby the better to know the world betimes, and to be able to go through with the fame, to the honor and feruice of their prince and countrie, and their owne wel-fare, and aduancement in the Common-wealth, whereof a very great number haue fhewed themfelues, and at this day many are very notable and beneficiall members. Befides, the faid Companie hath a Gouernour, or in his abfence, a Deputie, and

and foure and twentie Affiftantes in the Marte Towne, who haue iurifdiction, and full authoritie as wel from her Maieftie, as from the Princes, States and Rulers of the Low Countries, and beyond the feas, without Appeale, prouocation, or declination, to ende and determine all Ciuill caufes, queftions, and controuerfies arifing betweene or among the brethren, members, and fuppoftes of the faid Companie, or betweene them and others, either Englifh, or Straungers, who either may or will prorogate the Iurifdiction of the faid Companie, and their court, or are fubiect to the fame by the priuiledges, and Charters thereunto granted.

By the faid Gouernour and Affiftantes are alfo appointed, and chofen a Deputie, and certaine difcreet perfons, to be Affociates to the faid Deputie, in all other places conuenient, as well within, as without the realme of England, who all hold Correfpondence with the Gouernour of the Company, and chiefe Court in the Marte Towne on the other fide the feas, and haue fubalterne power to exercife Merchants law, to rule, and looke to the good ordering of the Brethren of the Companie euery where, as farre as may be, and their Charters will beare them out.

Further, the faid Company entertaineth godly and learned Preachers with liberall ftipendes, and other benefites: hath alfo Treafurers, Secretaries, and other needeful Officers, the end of all which is: *The feemely and orderly gouernment and rule of all the members, parts, and brethren of the fayd Company wherefoeuer in their Trade, and feate of Merchandife. Secondly, The preferuation of amitie, and the Enter courfe betweene the Realme of England and their Neighbours and Allies, and the preuenting of innouations, griefes, wronges, and exactions contrarie to the fame. Thirdly, The great vet, aduancemet, and keeping in eftimation of Englifh Commodities, and the bringing in of forreigne Commodities good cheape. Fourthly, The maintenance of the Nauigation. Fiftbly, The increafe of the Queenes Incomes and Cuftomes. Sixtly, and laftly, The honour, and feruice of the Prince, and of our State and Countrey, at home and abroad.*

*Benefites and Commodities arifing by the Companie of the Merchants Aduenturers.*

Now that al thefe benefites and commodities arife by the

Companie of Merchantes Aduenturers, I hope by and by, plainely to shew, and withall to proue, That by the said Company, all the abouewritten points are better performed and brought to passe, then if all were set at libertie as some haue desired, and consequently that without the said Company, few, or none of the aforesaid benefits or Commodities wil be so well raised or redounde to the State, & Common wealth.

*Of Rule, and Gouernment, the first point and Commoditie arising by the vnited Company of M.M. Aduenturers.*

 SHALL not need to say much in commendation of good Gouernment, and Policie, as hauing before touched the same in part, and shewed how needfull and requisite it is also in matter of Commerce, Trade, and the seat of Merchandise. Now that the Companie of Merchantes Aduenturers had for this point been anciently famous, and highly praised and esteemed of Strangers, as well as of those of their owne Countrey, and so continueth to this day (although much disturbed, and disquieted by new Tulles and Dimockes) I thinke no man doubteth, so that I take it as granted, that the State and Common wealth hereby reapeth more profit, then if men were suffered to run a loose, & irregular course without order, command, or ouersight of any: whereby many griefes, hurtes, dissentions, and inconueniences, besides no smal dishonour or the Prince, and State would in short time arise, as heretofore they haue done for want of sage and discreet gouernment, of which remedie seeing the aforesaid Companie is sufficiently prouided, and that it hath been by the experience of so many Ages, and the allowance of 11. Princes of the realme approued, me thinkes, it were an offence, and wrong vnto the State offered to goe about to alter, or hinder the same: *atq; ita Cornicũ oculos cõfigere*

*That*

*That the Amitie, and Entercourse betweene the Realme of*
England, *and their Neighbours, and Allies, are che-*
rished, *& all Innouations, griefes wrongs, and exacti-*
ons contrarie to the same, are preuented by the maintenance of the Companie of the M.M. Aduenturers.*

THere hath beene of old time, very straight alliance
and amitie betweene the Kings of England, and
Princes of the Low Countries, especially since the
gouernment of the said countries came to the hands
of the Dukes of *Burgundy*, & among the said Dukes, betweene
king *Henry* 5. and *Philip*, surnamed the *Good*, father to *Charles*
surnamed the *Warriour*, which *Charles* was slaine before the
towne of *Nantes*: This Duke *Philip* had almost from a childe
bene brought vp in the court of England, so that between the
said king and him, and their subiects, was a very firme league,
friendship, & entercourse, the causes whereof, and of the former amitie, and league betweene the kings of England from
K. *Ed.* 3. and the said Princes of the Low Countries, are rec-
koned to be three principally. First the ayd of the said Kings,
in the pursute of their iust title to the Crowne of France. Secondly, the safer keeping of *Calice*, and the territories thereabouts in the possession of the said Kings. And thirdly, The
nearenes of *Flanders, Brabant, Holland,* and *Zealand* vnto the
realme, and the commodious scituation thereof for the vent
of English comodities, in which Prouinces the English Mer-
chāts were at that time setled. This neighborly league grounded vpon the abouesaid causes hath constantly continued e-
uer since, but more nearely was confirmed betweene king
*Henrie* 5. and the abouesaid D. of *Burgundie*, who liued in the
yere of our L. 1420. so that since that time it hath neuer been
broken but at the death or change of any Prince, on each
part hath been renewed, confirmed, & sometime augmented
and namely betweene king *Henrie* 7. and king *Philip* sonne to
the Emperour *Maximiliane*, and father to *Charles* the fifth
Emperour, and for the maintenance, and cherishing of the

faid league, and entercourfe, it is well knowne to thofe which
are conuerfant in Hiftorie of things paft, that fince the win-
ning of *Calice*, by King *Edward* the third, in the yeere 1347.
The Kings of England haue with great Armies by lande,
and Fleetes of fhippes by fea, inuaded the Realme of France,
in the quarrel, and for the ayd of the Houfe of *Burgundie*, as
well as for their owne particular claymes, and right, and efpecially King *Henrie* the fifth, as appeareth by diuers writers of
thofe times, and fince : but to let paffe fo old matters, and onely to rehearfe fomewhat of that which hath bene done in the
memorie of men yet liuing, are not long before, I wil in briefe
recount fome fpeciall proofes of that abouefaid, giuing this
note by the way that as the Kings of England, and the Dukes
of *Burgundie* were ioyned in league and friendfhip, fo were
the French & Scots, that whenfoeuer England had warre with
France, Scotland had the like with England, fo that the Kings
of England haue had alwaies double warres with the French
and Scots together, & haue been forced from time to time to
keepe two Armies, fometimes three at once in the field.

*Aydes giuen by the Kings of England to the Houfe of Burgundie.*

In the yeere 1492. King *Henrie* the feuenth, in fauour and
ayd of *Maximiliane*, Archduke of *Auftrich*, and fonne to
the Emperour *Fredericke* the fourth, who had maried the Ladie *Marie*, daughter and fole heire to *Charles* the Warriour,
flaine before *Nantz*, as aforefaid, and againft whom almoft
all the Townes in Flanders rebelled and tooke armes, and
with the ayd of the French befieged the Towne of *Dixmyde*,
the faid King fent ouer the Lord *Dawbenye*, and the Lord
*Morley*, with an Army vpon his owne charges into Flanders,
who raifed the aforefaid fiege & flew eight thoufad Frenchmen & Flemmings in the place, taking all their prouifion and
ordinance: & in the yere following, when *Nieuport*, a Towne
lying vpon the fea-coft of Flanders was befieged by Monfi-
eur de *Cordes* a French man, with twentie thoufand French
and Flemings, & that one of the principalleft Towers or Bul-
warks of the faid towne was entred, & held by the enemy, yet
by the valiant refiftace of fuch Englifh men as were within it,
and frefh fupply fent by the aforefaid king the forefaid *Cordes*

was

was forced to leaue the faid Towne with fhame, and loffe of many of his men, and much prouifion. In the fame yeare alfo, the faid King *Henry* the feuenth fent an Armie by fea vnder the conduct of the Lord *Pominges*, to the aid of the faid Archduke *Maximilian*, againft the Lord of *Rauenftein*, Generall of the rebellious Flemings, who had taken the Caftle & Towne of *Slufe* (the onely Hauen and Port to the feas of that old and famous Towne of *Bridges*) but the Lord *Pomings* recouered the faid Caftle by force, and deliuered it to *Albert* Duke of *Saxonie*, Generall for the forefaid Archduke. By the fauing of which Caftle, and the abouefaid Towne of *Newport*, the whole Earldome of Flanders was faued out of the hands of the French King, who otherwife, without the aide of King *Henrie* of England, had ioyned the fame to the Crowne of France. In the yeare following, the faid King *Henrie*, in reuenge of the great fcorne and iniurie done to the abouefaid Archduke by the French King, partly in returning home the Ladie *Margaret*, daughter to the faid Archduke, who was affianced, and after the maner of great Princes, by Deputies maried to the faid French King, and partly by getting in craftie fort the Ladie *Anne*, the only heire of the Dutchie of *Britanie* from the faid Archduke, to whom fhe was maried, entered France with a great Armie, where the faid Archduke promifed to meete him with another Armie on his part, and although the faid promife was not kept, yet the faid king proceeded on his purpofe, befieged *Bullen*, and finally, conftrained the French King to feeke peace of him, and to giue him a great fumme of money, with the which (and great fpoyle got by his people) he returned into England, to his high honour and praife, without once feeing or hauing any helpe at all of the fayd *Maximilian*.

In the yeare 1512. at which time the French King made warres with *Ferdinando* King of Spaine, & inuaded his Countries by land, King *Henrie* the eight (of famous memorie) fent an aid of tenne thoufand men by fea into Spaine, vnder the leading of the Noble Lord, the Lord *Thomas Grey* Marquis Dorfed, at the requeft of the aboue mentioned *Maximilian*,

then

then Emperour, whose only sonne and heire *Philip* had married *Ioan*, the daughter and heire of the abouesaid *Ferdinando*. Two yeares after this, the said King *Henrie*, in fauour and defence of the young Prince or infant of Spaine, *Charles*, grandchild to the abouesaid *Maximilian*, and afterwards Emperour himselfe, went ouer in person with a mightie armie into France, and besieged the strong Towne of *Terwin*, which finally was yeelded vnto him, maugre the whole power of Fraunce: after he had discomfited and ouerthrowne in battell the French Armie, slaying eight or tenne thousand in the place, and taking prisoners the Duke *de Longueville*, the Marquisse *Retelois*, and besides, 240. Lords, Knights, and Gentlemen of name and honour. In which battell the abouesaid Emperour with at least fortie or fiftie of the Nobilitie of the low Countries, serued vnder the Kings Standerd, receiuing wages of him, and wearing the red Crosse or Cognizance of England. After the rendring ouer of *Terwin*, the said King brought his Armie before the Citie of *Tournay*, or *Dornick*, at that time termed the Maiden Citie (for that it neuer had beene wonne by Prince) but King *Henrie* got it, and hauing taken order for the sure keeping thereof, returned the way that he came, being a long martch of 63. miles with great honour and glorie, into England. And in the meane while the Duke of *Norfolke*, and his sonne the Earle of *Surry* had discomfited an armie of fiftie thousand Scots, vnder the leading of their King *Iames* the fourth, who was slaine in the field with fourteene thousand of his people, whereof many were of the Nobilitie, besides 12. Earles, 20. Lords, 40. or 50. knights, and many Gentlemen taken prisoners.

In the yeare 1514. the said king *Henrie* the eight did send a band of 1500. choise souldiours, vnder the leading of the Lord *Clinton*, vnto the aide of the Lady *Margaret*, Regent of the low Countries against the Duke of Gelderland.

In the yeare 1530. a perpetuall peace was agreed vpon, and sworn at *Paris* in France, betwixt the Emperour *Charles* the fifth, the king of England, and the French king, during their three liues: and which of the three should first violate, or breake this peace, the other two were bounde to set vpon him, as their open and ioynt enemie: this peace was first broken on the French kings part, by reason of a quarrell betweene the Emperour and the said king, whereupon the king of England, for his oath and promise sake, sent ouer into France a great Armie, vnder the leading of the Duke of *Suffolke*, and prepared a great Fleet of ships by sea, to annoy the said Countrie, & by this meanes drew the Scots against him: for the Duke of *Albany* in ayd of the French entred England, and began to spoile the borders thereof, against whom the Earle of *Surrey* was sent, who forced the Scots to retire, to their great losse and dishonour, and entred Scotland at their heeles, burning and spoiling the Country afore him, and returning with great praie and bootie.

In the yeare 1543. the said king *Henry* the eight sent ouer Sir *Iohn Wallop*, and other Gentlemen, with a band of sixe thousand men, to the aide of the foresaid Emperor *Charles*, when he went to *Landersey*. And in the yeare 1545. the said king in person with two Armies went ouer into Fraunce, in aide of the said Emperour *Charles*, at which time he besieged and tooke *Bullen*: but how ill the said Emperour kept promise with the said king, & afterward without his knowledge or priuity, made peace with the French king, I shall not need to say much, as being pardy fresh in mans memorie, & partly commended to writing by such as liued in those dayes. *Sleidans's lib. 6.*

In the yeare 1557. Queene *Marie* in fauour of her husband king *Philip*, and by his procurement and meanes, made warres vpon Fraunce, sending ouer an Armie by sea, vnder the Lord *Clinton*, high Admirall of England, into Britanie, where they landed, spoyled, and burnt a great way into the Countrey: And another Armie of ten thousand men by land, vnder the Earles of *Penbroke*, *Bedford*, and *Rutland*, by whose help king *Philip* got the strong Towne of *S. Quintins*, & had his will of the French king. But the English by these warres, and breaking peace with France for king *Philips* sake, lost the Towne of *Calice*, which the predecessors of the said Queene had kept in spight of all France 210. yeares before that time.

What

What other priuie helpes Queene *Marie* gaue vnto her fayd Husband, few or none can tell, but it is thought, he had many an hundred thousand pounds from her, that all the world knew not of. These warres haue the kings of England taken in hand, and these aydes from time to time haue they giuen to the house of *Burgundie*, besides great, and vnknowne summes of money lent, in so much, that in the opinion of men of knowledge and experience, it cost the Realme of England three score times an hundred thousand pounds at least, in the quarrell and defence of the Princes of the said house, within the compasse of 76. yeares after that *Maximilian* maried with the Lady *Marie*, daughter to *Charles* the *Warriour*, and heire to the said house. To say nothing of that which happened before, and now of late hath fallen out since the troubles in the low Countries, in all which the Kings & Queenes of England haue shewed themselues faithfull and friendly Princes, and good Neighbours and Allies to the said low Countries, and truly and readily haue holpen, and stood by the Princes thereof in their greatest neede and extremitie: whereas we cannot reade, that those of the house of *Burgundy* euer made warres against Scotland, or France, in helpe of the Kings of England directly: neither were they or any of them euer required thereunto but once, and that was in the dayes of King *Edward* the sixt, being then but eight or nine yeares of age, and at such time as he had both warre with Scotland and France at once, and besides was troubled with a great rebellion of his subiects at home: for which cause a solemne Embassage was sent to the Emperour *Charles* the fifth, who layd before the said Emperour the feeble estate of the said King *Edwards* infancie and tender yeares, and the commotion of his subiects, euen vpon the neck of the warres & troubles with Fraunce and Scotland, putting the said Emperour in mind of the great Armies, which at sundrie times had beene sent out of England in aid of his father, and grandfather, and also of the dangerous and chargeable warres begun, and taken in hand by King *Henrie* the eight, the saide Kings father, for the quarrell of the said Emperour alone, as then but an infant

*Embassage to the Emperour Charles the fifth from King Edward the sixth.*

fant also, and vnder yeares : they did not let further to tel him
of the great paines and trauel taken by the said K. *Henrie*, with
his friends the Princes Electors, & others of Germany, at the
request of the said Emperour, to preferre him to the Imperial
Crowne and Dignitie, which he now possessed and perhaps
might els haue missed. Lastly, they prayed the said Emperour
to remember the ancient and faithfully continued amitie betweene the Emperour and his predecessours, Dukes of Burgundie, and the predecessors of the said King *Edward*, & that
the warres which he now had with Scotland and France, was
for none other cause moued, then in maintenance of the said
Amitie, and in defence of the Quarrell of the house of Burgundie, and at the request of the Princes thereof onely. But
as the said Emperour had dealt before with Duke *Frederick*
of Saxonie, by whose meanes especially he attained to the
Imperiall Dignitie, so he did the like with King *Edward* :
for cleane forgetting all old and new friendship, he gaue the
Embassadours vncourteous words, for the alteration of the
Religion by their King, and would do nothing, except the
same were changed againe into the olde. Whereupon they
besought the said Emperour, that he would at least be pleased
to take into his hands and keeping the Towne of *Bullen*, not
long before got from France by King *Henrie* the eight, and
that but for a time, till the said King *Edward* had quieted the
troubles with his subiects at home. But this he wold not yeeld
vnto neither, except the King would change his Religion:
which the King and his Counsell (hauing the feare of God
before their eies) vtterly refused, chusing rather to lose earth-
ly things, then heauenly : and therefore seeing the Emperour
would neither giue aide himselfe, nor suffer anie munition or
souldiors to go out of his land into England, no not so much
as an armor (as I haue hard) that one of the Embassaders had
bought for himselfe at *Brusselles*, a peace in the yeare 1549
was concluded with France and Scotland, with the restoring
of *Bullen*, and vpon other conditions according to the time :
This peace fell out but little to the profite of the Emperour,
for in the yeare 1551. beganne the great warres betweene

E                              him

him, and *Henrie* the French king, wherein the Burgundians felt the want of their old truflie friends and Allies the king of England, and his people. And vndoubtedly, if the kings of England had not continually aided and aſſiſted the houſe of Burgundie, & the low Countries, they had both been French before this day : or if the French King might haue beene ſure of England, and without feare thereof bent his whole forces by ſea, and by land againſt the houſe of *Burgundie*, & Spaine, neither ſhould the Emperor haue got ſo much aduantage, as he did againſt the French king, neither haue bin able to haue troubled Germany, & the Germane Princes, nor other Princes, States, & countries, as he did, neither ſhould he haue gotten ſo much poſſeſſion & dominion in Italy, and other places, as he got, neither laſtly, ſhould his ſubiects haue obtained ſo great wealth & riches, nor ſo much knowledge by land and ſea, as they haue done. For ſurely, he, and his people may thanke the Kings of England for all theſe things: for the ayd of the ſaid Kings, and the traffique and reſort of the Engliſh Merchants haue bin the principall cauſes thereof: & therfore great reaſon had the Dukes of Burgundy to ſeeke the friendſhip and amitie of the Kings of England, and to cheriſh and augment the ſame by Treaties, and Entercourſe from time to time, which are yet continued in force : and whereof the foreſaid Company of Merchants Aduenturers, haue ſo good notice, record, and vnderſtanding, that vpon anie occaſion whatſoeuer, they haue them ready, therby to defend the right of the Realme, and ſubiects thereof, againſt ſuch as would either wilfully, or vnawares breake and violate the ſame, which ought to remaine as ſacred, and vntouched, for the preſeruation of mutuall friendſhip and amitie betweene both nations, which oftentimes for want of due care, and prouiſion on this behalfe in time, might turne into open enmitie, and alienation of good will, not without daunger of warre in the end, if ſome men might haue their willes. As in the yeare

*Don Giraldo Deſpes.*

1564. *Don Giraldo Deſpes* Embaſſador for the king of Spaine in England, at the inſtance of the Cardinall *Granvelle*, dealt with a Stranger, yet liuing in England, and well knowne there

there, to draw out a summarie of all the doleances of the low Country Merchants, promising redresse therein, or to bring the matter to an open warre : which whether the said stranger did or not, I cannot iustly say, but it is like enough his busie head considered, and he hath conceiued no small discontentment of old, that things go not, as he would faine haue them in England, for his owne particular fancies sake, and employment, without regarding the alteration of times, or breach of Amitie, which might fall out betweene her Maiestie and the States of the vnited low Countries for that cause, so he might come to his purpose. For immediately vpon this followed that violent procceding of the Dutchesse of *Parma,* in banishing of English Cloth and Commodities out of the low Countries, by means whereof, the Commerce and trade for a time surceased, not without perill of warre betweene the Princes and their people. The Companie therefore of the Merchants Aduenturers are a great obstacle to the raising and bringing in of new, and vnwonted Tolles, Imposts, exactions, and grieuances, which otherwise the subiects of the Realme of England, their ships and goods would bee charged with, and oppressed, contrarie to the Treaties of Amity, and Entercourses, to the empouerishing of the said subiects, and the hinderance of the Nauigation : which commeth to passe by meanes and helpe of their common purse, and by officers maintained to keepe regitter of all things needfull, and to defend these common causes from time to time, when any Innouation or strange exaction is brought in, tending to the hurt & hindrance of the Merchants, Mariners, and seafaring men, and consequently, to the dammage and preiudice of the whole state. And this a particular man is not able to do, for either his purse, or meanes will not reach vnto it, or else being loth to spend his money and time, or to hinder his affaires, and trade hereabouts, will rather yeelde vnto a wrong: whereby it commeth to passe by little & little, that the ancient rights of the Realme are either lessened, or infringed, & that, which ought not to be suffered, vnwonted tallages, taxes, and impositions, are leuied vpon the subiects,

to.

to his great grieuance, and empouerishing, and to the bringing of the Trade into strangers hands only : a thing of long
time practised, and laboured for by them, & chiefly preuented and withstood by the Companie of Merchants Aduenturers : which hath stirred vp the Easterlings, and some Merchants of *Antwerp* of late dayes against them : the Easterlings
continue still in their pride of heart and indurate malice, the
Antwerpians and their new-borne Colledge (the troubles
growing vpon them) were forced to be quiet, though within
these three yeeres, their first and last (perhaps) Consul, and
Secretarie haue sollicited the States Generall of the vnited
Prouinces with their complaints and accusations to embrace
and renew their old quarrels and pretences, and to set vp on
foote againe their decayed Consulate, in recompence of the
good seruices heretofore done (which I could wish examined, for that they vaunt themselues thereof) and for the great
benefite, that may hereafter redound to the said vnited lands
by the same, as they would haue the said States beleeue. The
true purpose and drift whereof is nothing els (as I said) but
to eat the Aduenturers out of their trade, as they of *Antwerp*

The Antwerpians
eate the Mer-
chants of other
Nations out of
their trade.

heretofore did the Merchants of other nations, Portugals, Italians, Dutches or Germans, and others, whereby they greatly
enriched themselues, their prince and countrey : which finally turned to the hurt, danger, & disquieting of all other Princes and States, as hath appeared by the doings and practises
of the late King *Philip* of Spaine, and his Confederates. And
to shew that this which I haue said is true, I will by the way
more particularly rip vp this matter.

First, for the Portingall, we know, that like a good simple
man, he sayled euerie yeare full hungerly (God wot) about
3. parts of the earth almost for spices, & when he had brought
them home , the great rich purses of the Antwerpians, subie-
iects of the King of Spaine, ingrossed them all into their own
hands, yea oftentimes gaue money for them before hand,
making thereof a plaine Monopoly : whereby they only gained, and all other nations lost. For that the spices, being in few
mens handes, were sold at such a rate, as they listed, to their
owne

owne priuate lucre and gaine, and to the hurt and damage of all others.

The Italians, English and Germane Merchantes, were wont to haue a very profitable, and good trade into Italie with Kerſyes, and other English, and forreigne commodities ſeruing that Countrey, but a litle before the troubles of the Low Countryes, the Antwerpians were growne into that trade, and were become the greateſt dealers that way, and further, to *Alexandria, Cypres, Tripolie in Siria,* and other remote places ſeruing the ſame more then any other, with linnen cloth, Worſteds, Sayes, Tapeſtrie, & other Netherlandiſh wares, by meanes whereof the ſaid Italians, English and Germanes were forced to leaue that trade, or to doe very little.

The Dutch or Germane Merchants had the whole trade in their owne handes, of all Commodities brought to *Antwerpe* from other places, that ſerued Germanie, buying vp all themſelues, and carying them to the Townes and Martes in their owne Countrey: but in a few yeeres the Antwerpians had alſo wholy got that trade, and the Germanes in a maner, did nothing, for the other in all the Marts, & Faires in Dutchland, bare the chiefeſt ſwindge, and ſerued the ſame with Commodities of all Landes, and of all ſorts, ſo that looke what the Germane vſed to get, that they got, eating as it were the bread out of his mouth.

As for the *Eaſterlings,* they had begun a Staple of their Commodities at *Antwerpe,* but in the opinion of wiſe men, if it had long continued, it would haue eaten out cleane, and conſumed their Marchantes and Marriners from the Seas, as they beganne not alitle to be diminiſhed by thoſe of *Amſterdam,* and other, but new vpſtarte townes in Holland, with their great number of Hulkes, and other Shippes: of the Spaniſh trade, and Merchantes of Spaine, becauſe they were King *Philips* ſubiects, there is not ſo much to be ſaid, but yet the Antwerpians had meanes, to get a good fleece from them too: for the Merchantes of *Antwerpe* beeing of great wealth, were able to ſell thoſe Commodities, which beſt ſerued Spaine, and the Indies, at long dayes of payment, and by

meanes

meanes thereof did set them at such high, and deare prices,
that when the dayes of payment came, and the Spaniard lac-
ked his returnes, to keepe credite with, hee was forced to run
vpon the Exchange, or Interest, till his prouision came in, by
which time his gaines was consumed by vsurie, and many
times some of the principall: besides, they sold the Spaniard
their worst wares, and carryed the choysest themselues into
Spaine, whether they traded more, then all the Spaniards in
the land did. For the trade of the Marchants of France: there
hath beene often warre betweene that Countrey and the
Dukes of *Burgundie*, as hath been aboue partly touched,
by meanes whereof, there hath beene much colouring of
good between the one Princes people & the other, and that
so ordinarily, and cunningly, that the *Antwerpians* aboue
all the Marchants besides, were as priuie, expert, and skilfull
in all the French trickes, and indirect trades and conueyan-
ces, as the Frenchmen themselues, by reason whereof in time
of peace the French Merchants were much endamaged, and
hindred: for the *Antwerpians* serued Germanie, Spaine, Por-
tingale, Estland, and their neighbours of the Lowe Countries, with such things as the Frenchmen themselues vsed to
sell, and vent in those places: Now let vs looke a while into
England and take a view, what the *Antwerpians* and other
Netherlanders, principally those of *Antwerpe*, haue done
there, and you shall find that not past 80. yeeres agoe, there
were not in all *London* aboue twelue or sixteene Low Countrie Marchants, and amongst them not past foure of any credite, or estimation. For the Merchandise which they then
brought into England most, were stone pottes, brushes, pup-
pets, and toyes for children, bristles for shoomakers, and such
other pedlery ware of small valew, and sometimes a litle fish,
and three or foure peeces of linnen cloth, but in lesse then the
compasse of fortie yeres following, there were in *London*, at
least one hundred Netherlandish Merchantes, the most part
whereof were of *Antwerpe*, and thither they brought all
kinde of wares, which the Merchantes of Italie, Germanie,
Spaine, France, and Eastland (of all which nations there were
before

before that time diuers famous and notable rich Merchants
and Companies) vſed to bring into England out of their own
Countries directly, to the great damage of the ſaid ſtrangers,
and of the naturall borne English Marchants, which English
Merchants and their trade alſo the Netherlanders (but eſpecially thoſe of *Antwerpe*) as much as in them laye, euen then
ſought, and practiſed to deſtroy, and ouerthrowe, and ſince
hath beene many yeres about it, which in good time was diſ-
couered, and by diligence and trauaile of the Merchants Aduenturers principally, not without their great coſt and charge
hath been hitherto withſtood and preuented, and ſo will bee
ſtill ſo long, as that Companie continueth on foot, let the o-
ther repine and mutter at it, as much as they liſt, and ſeeke to
croſſe and hinder the Aduenturers whereſoeuer they can
procure audience with their vnſeaſonable Remonſtrances,
ſpitefull Declarations, & harſh Complaints, to the raiſing vp,
as much as in them lyeth, of the like ſtirre and diſagreement
betweene her Maieſtie, and the States of the vnited Nether-
lands, at this time, as happened in the yeere 1563. vnder the
gouernment of the Dutcheſſe of *Parma*, Regent for the late
king *Philip* of Spaine, at that time in the Lowe Countryes:
when as through the complaint of the Merchants of *Antwerp*
principally & of others of the ſaid Low Countries, againſt the
raiſing of the Cuſtome of cloth, & of forreigne wares, brought
into England, & ſpecially againſt an Act of Parliament made
for the ſetting of her Maieſties people on worke, by vertue
wherof forreign wares, as pinnes, kniues, hats, girdles, ribbin,
and ſuch like, were forbiddē to be brought in ready wrought,
to the intent, that her Highnes ſubiects might be imployed in
making therof, the ſaid Dutches of *Parma* by proclamatiō for
bad the carying into Englād of any kinde of matter, or thing,
wherwith the ſaid wares might be made, & baniſhed out of
the Low Countries all *Manufacture*, or handywork, as baves,
&c. made in England, cloth & kerſve only excepted, which
alſo ſhe afterwardes forbad to bee brought in vpon paine of
confiſcation, vnder ſhew, or pretence of infection, (for that
the plague had reigned very ſore in *London* & other places of
the

the Realme that Summer) but in very trueth the right cause
was, for that she could not haue her will in the aboue mentioned points, and tooke that time of mortalitie, & want of trade
in England to be the readiest and fittest opportunitie to at-
taine thereunto. So that finally the Merchants Aduenturers,
after they had kept their Clothes & other goods aboord their
ships in the Riuer of *Thames*, and *Scheld* fiue moneths together and might not be permitted to land them at *Antwerpe*,
were at length forced to depart with the same vnto the towne
of *Embden*, in Eastfriseland, where they obteined priuiledges
and contracted for a free Commerce with the two yong
Earles *Egdard* and *Iohn*, and the Lady *Anne* Countesse of *Ol-
denburghe* their Mother Anno 1564. who neither feared nor
found any contagion in the English and their Commodities,
and by this meanes brake the violence of the aforesaid Dut-
chesses intention, erecting their trade in the aboue said town,
and leauing *Antwerpe* and the Low Countries, whereupon
King *Philip* and his ministers grieued sore that they could not
haue their will of her Maiestie, and her Highnesse subiectes,
and that they must forgoe so profitable a Milch-cowe as the
English Trade was vnto the Lowe Counties: an Edict or
Proclamation was set foorth in the Moneth of Maye of the a-
bousaid yeere, That no person in the saide Lowe Countries
should haue, or vse any Trade with the English at *Embden*,
buy any Cloth or English Woollen Commoditie of them, or
carry them any wares vpon paine of confiscation of the same:
then the which dealing what could be more iniurious, or e-
nemy-like in time of open warres? But herein the said King
not onely shot at the State of England, but withall bee en-
dammaged other Nations, and particularly those of the Empire, as though no Countrie Merchantes ought to trade any
where, but in his Countries, and when, and where, and with
whom it pleased him, thereby to hold all the whole trade of
Merchandise in his Netherlads alone, forbidding vpon paine
of losse of goods the Imperiall Merchantes, as well as others,
from occupying, buying or selling within the limites of the
Empire, as though he had been Emperour himselfe, and more
                   then

*Prohibition of all
Trade with the
English by king
Philip.*

then Emperour: In which point hee touched very neare the top and height of the Emperiall Crowne and Dignitie, in that being but Duke of *Burgundie*, & that in respect but a subiect of the Empire, he tooke vpon him peremptorily, to command, restraine, forbid, and iniuriously to breake the old, and ancient freedoms, and liberties of the Empire freely yeelded, and so long religiously maintained and kept, as well toward all the subiects, as towardes all the friendes and Allies of the same, amongst which friends the English haue been continually not the least, or last, as fetching their originall out of the said holy Empire. At length when the king of Spaine, for all the instigation of the Netherlanders and popish ministers, saw that hee could not preuaile, and were at a stand, hee and they were glad and fayne to come to a prouisionall agreement, and to accept of such priuiledges and liberties, as the said Netherlanders enioyed in England in the last yeere of Q. *Maries* reigne: which was the yere of our L. 1558. and to call in all those foresaid Placates, Edictes and Prohibitions, made against the English and bringing in of English wares.

And although in the yeere following, and the yere 1566. a diete was held at *Bridges*, for the taking vp, and compounding of all variances difficulties and greiuances, by certaine Embassadours sent from both Princes, yet nothing was concluded, the Custome about the which the first and most question grew, were for al the Netherlandish Merchants wrangling and importunitie continued, as hauing beene erected in Queene *Maries* dayes (King *Philip* their naturall prince being married to her) and the former agreement made in the yeere 1564. between the Queenes Counsell and Don *Gusman de Silua* Embassadour for the aboue said king stoode, and so remayned in force til the yere 1568. when as the D. of *Alua* in the Low Countries, and king *Philip* throughout Spaine caused the persons, and goods of the English Merchantes, to be arrested, and stayed vpon this occasion: it happened in the abouesaid yeere 1568. that a great ship of *Biscaie*, and foure pinasses which the Spaniards call *Assabres*, were chased by certaine men of warre belonging to the Prince of *Conde*, into

the

the Hauen of *Plimmoth* : in which great ship were the valew
of two hundred thousand Pistolettes, which money the Spanish Embassadour at that time in England, *Don Giraldo De-*
*spes*,required to haue deliuered to him, as belonging to the
king his Master, with consent to conueigh the same to *Ant-*
*werpe* vnto the Duke of *Alua*, which was granted him, but
while he attended order fró the said Duke, about the safe sending of the said money, her Maiestie came to the knowledge
that it did not belong to the king of Spaine, but vnto certaine
Merchants of *Genua*, & that the Duke of *Alua* needing money, meant to seaze vpon the same, and turne it to the K.vse.
Which the owners fearing, chose rather, that it should remaine in the Queenes hands. Whereupon,her Maiestie caused all the money to be landed,saying that she would borow
it of the Italians,with their good will and liking, and so preserue it from the French, who threatned to fetch it by force
out of the Hauen where it lay. The Duke as soone as hee had
knowledge thereof,suddenly commanded all the Merchants
Aduenturers to be arrested at *Antwerpe*,and caused them to
be kept safe in the English house, with a company of Dutch
souldiers: he commanded also the ships and goods of all the
English Merchants as well at *Antwerpe* as elsewhere, to be
attached,and inuentarised,which he afterwards sold to *Fer-*
*nando Frias* a Spaniard & others,to the vse of the K.of Spaine.
When her Maiestie vnderstood of this hastie and vnaduised
dealing of the D. *Alua*,she gaue leaue vnto her Subiects for
their Indempnitie,to arrest the Netherlanders & their goods
in England: By the meanes of these generall arrestes on both
sides,the trade of the M.M.Aduenturers ceased at *Antwerp*,
but for the sale of the commoditie of the land, they presently
contracted with the Towne of *Hamborough*, and there helde
their Martes onely for a time: The Duke of *Alua* on the o-
ther side to hinder the trade, and consequently to hurt the
State of England,the last day of March 1569.by straight proclamation forbad all dealing with the English, either in carrying them any wares,or buying of them English commodities,to be brought into the low Countries,appointing for the
more

*The Duke of Al-*
*ua arresteth the*
*persons and goods*
*of the English in*
*Antwerpe and*
*elsewhere in the*
*Low Countreys.*

more seuere execution thereof certaine spyes, or promoters, among the which as principall, was Doctor *Storie*, of whose shamefull & weldeserued punishment & end, there is yet fresh memory; but these differences and troubles, were afterwards in the yere 1574. at a Diete held at *Bristow* taken vp & agreed, & the Entercourse was renewed & confirmed in such maner, as was concluded at *Bridges* in the yeere 66. to the high honour and commendation of her Maiestie, who medled not with one penie of the arrestes goods, but gaue the same wholy ouer vnto her subiects, in recompence of their losses in the low Countries, and honourably contented the owners of the money (about the which the question & trouble first arose) for the same: Whereas to the contrary the king of Spaine neuer recompenced his subiectes for their damages, but as is said, conuerted all the English Marchants goods, which hee found in the low Countries or in Spaine to his owne vse, without hauing the least consideration of the losse of any man. By the abouewritten discourse wee may perceiue the sleightes, practises, & industrie of the *Antwerpians*, and Netherlanders, to drawe the trades of all nations into their owne handes, the proud, vnneighbourly, yea enemilike Edictes and Proscriptions of the Dutchesse of *Parma*, vpon the vnreasonable complaintes & demands of her Merchants, no doubt egged on by the Cardinall *Granuelle* in hatred of the Religion professed in England: the rash & vnaduised arrests, & detaining of the persons, and goods of the M. M. Aduentures & others in the Low Countries, and Spaine, by the K. and the D. of *Alua*: the Heroicall courage, wisedome, and equitie of our gratious Queen in defence, and reliefe of her subiect, wronged & spoyled in barbarous sort, contrary to reason, & against the Entercourse, and Treaties sworne, and established between both nations, and the Princes thereof: And lastly the great care, & trauaile of the M. M. Aduenturers in the middest of all these troubles, and their exceeding great losses, & hinderances, to seek, and procure a place, First at *Embde*, then at *Hamborough*, for vent of the commoditie of the realme, and maintenance of the trade, wherby so many liue, the ouerthrow and destruction wherof,

hath been the principall marke and purpose of all the aboue
mentioned complaints, edicts, proscriptions, and arrests, and
is now at this day of all the violent machinations, and work-
ings of the king of Spaine, and his ministers and fauourers (to
which partie the *Hanses* adioyne themselues with might and
mayne) thinking thereby to stirre vp some notable commotion, trouble or disorder in the State of England, and so
the sooner to bring to passe their long purposed bloody, and
treacherous practises against the precious life of her Maiestie,
(whom the Lord long preserue amongst vs) and against the
true Religion, and Church of CHRIST planted in her Highnesse Dominions, and in steed thereof to set strangers ouer
vs and to reestablish poperie, and so lastly, bring the whole
English people and subiectes of her Maiestie into miserable
slauerie of bodie and conscience, vnder an vngodly and su-
perstitious nation, from the which the Almighty GOD in
mercy keepe vs, and our posteritie, that wee may see peace
in our dayes, and that there may bee rest in the Church vnto
the end of the world. But to returne to my purpose.

---

*That the better and greater vent and aduancement of Eng-*
*lish Commodities, and the bringing in of forreigne wares*
*(good cheape) is procured by the Company of Merchants*
*Aduenturers.*

HE next benefite which ariseth to the
Prince and State by the maintenance of
the Companie of the Marchantes Aduenturers is, The better and greater vent,
and aduancement of English Commodities, and the bringing in good cheape of
forreigne wares. Which to be so, not onely, that which hath
passed heretofore, but also fresh experience hath sufficiently
manifested: for first it is plaine, as hath been aboue touched,
that in times long past, and euen of late yeeres, the M.M. Aduenturers did settle themselues in some one towne of the low
Countries, and there stapling the Woollen cloth, kersyes and

ether

other the commodities of the Realme of England, in good and merchantlike order, and vnder good & prudent Gouernment, did attend the Merchants strangers, which should repaire vnto the said Town (comonly termed the Mart Town) to buy the said Clothes, Kersies, &c. or to sel, or barter vnto the Merchants Aduenturers such forreigne commodities, as were most fit, and necessarie for the Realme of England, by means wherof great numbers of Merchants of Eastland, Germany, Italy, and almost out of all the Townes and Prouinces of the lowe Countries, resorted to that mart town: and there in most ample, friendly, and merchantlike maner did traffike, & deale with the said M.M. Aduenturers, whereby the English Commodities were kept and holden in singular credit & estimation, & all kind of forreigne wares were returned, & brought in at reasonable & low prices, not onely to the good of the Common wealth of England in generall, and the benefite of the M.M. Aduenturers in particular, but also to the great satisfaction, contentment, & good liking of all the aboue said forreigne States & people: insomuch, that some great personages, drawne with the verie report of the seemly dealing, cariage, & orders of the Company of M.M. Aduēturers, haue repaired to the Mart Towne, to behold & see the same.

This course deriued from common reason, and approued by Experience (the surest Doctor in the schoole of mans life) many yeeres together hath beene obserued, and continued in the aboue said Company, as a principal point, & one of the maine postes, & pillers of the same. For first, it cannot be denied, that to aduance any thing, & to make it of price and estimation, is to bring it in request: Secondly, to bring it in request, is to draw a concourse & multitude to desire it: And lastly, the best means to draw a Concourse & multitude, is to appoint a certaine place, whither men may commodiously resort, where also if they may find, not onely that which they desire & haue need of, but withall may vent that which their Countrie bringeth forth, and hath plentie of, it is a double cause & allurement to inuite them to such concourse and flocking together. From this reason is the order & institution

F 3 of

of the Mart-Towne fo long, and fo ferioufly practifed and
maintoined by the Merchant Aduéturers, which to be found-
ly and well grounded, I thinke no man will gainfay : next,
late expererience as well at home, as abroad, hath taught vs,
that when another courfe was liked of by fome, & that diuers
of the Company had disbanded themfelues, and held not the
aforefaid commendable & Merchantlike courfe, but erected
vnto themfelues a priuate, irregular, and ftragling Trade, the
commoditie of the Realme lay vnuented, or grew to be em-
bafed, & fold at lower prices then before. For when as about
fourteen yeares paft, in the 29th yere of her Maiefties reigne,

the Wool growers, Clothiers, Weauers, and others liuing
vpon Cloth making, wanting their accuftomed commodity,
gaines, and worke, made a grieuous complaint thereof, it
was thought to be the only expedient to remedy this fore, to
giue libertie to all her Highneffe fubiects, and others, to buy
and tranfport Cloth, according to the limitation of the lawes,
anie grants or priuiledges by her Maiefties Prerogatiue heretofore to the Merchants Aduenturers graunted notwithftan-
ding : yet we faw, that the maladie was neuer a whit the better, but rather grew worfe & worfe, infomuch that the poore
people in *Wiltfhiere* and *Glocefterfhiere*, liuing wholly vppon
Cloth-making, in great numbers were readie to growe into
a mutinie for this caufe, to the fingular reioycing of the enemies of her Maieftie, and in particular of the *Hanfes*, who defire nothing more, then the ouerthrowe of the M. M. Aduen-
rers and their Trade : thereby finally entending to difturbe
the peace of the whole Realme. At length, when all men expected nothing elfe but an abolifhment, and diffoluing of the
abouefaid Companie, as the fole and onely caufe of all this
griefe, the fetting vp of the Steelyard againe, & the equalling
of all the fubiects, and others in the Realme, in tranfporting,
and carrying out of Cloth : none of all thefe things fell out,
but to the contrarie, thofe of the faid Company were fent for,
and after they had beene heard, and had made knowne the
true caufe of the abouefaid fore indeed, they were willed to
proceed in their trade, with promife of affiftance, and countenance

tenance from my Lords, and others of the Counsell: which
assuredlie their Honors would not haue done, if that they had
seene, that the late innouation or libertie had brought forth,
or was likely to bring forth the promised effect: or that without the said Companie of Merchants Aduenturers, so great a
quantitie of the woollen commodities of the Realme could
be vented, as in former times, when the said Merchants Aduenturers were maintained, and backed in their ful Priuiledges and Rights.

THe Merchants Aduenturers were at this time encom-
bred with no small difficulties: for that neither of their
Mart-Townes (*Embden* and *Middelburgh*) were very safe,
or fit for the vtterance of their Commodities, neither knewe
they where to find a place conuenient for that purpose. For at
*Middelbourgh*, partly through the continuall loanes of great
summes of money, vpon the necke one of another required
at their hands, without warrant or authoritie from her Maiestie, and partly through the feare of danger they were put in
by the Earle of *Leicester*, then Gouernour of the vnited prouinces, the Trade was in a maner wholy damped, and diuerse
of the principallest of the Companie in that place, almost in
flying maner, withdrew themselues & their goods into Holland. At *Embden* on the other side, things were in no verie
good tearmes, by reason of the Duke of *Parmaes* preuailing
in the prouinces next adioyning, and that the States sent their
men of warre into the riuer of *Embs*, whereby the trade by
land grew exceeding perillous, and by water troublesome
& chargeable: some also to mend the matter, sticked not to
put into mens minds a suspition of the Count *Egdard* of *Eastfriseland*, as a secret Pensioner & fauorer of the King of Spain:
and sure it is, that his chiefe Officer *Ocko Freez*, then Drossart
of *Embden*, shewed himselfe by many signes & actions, verie
much inclined to the Spanish part. The *Hanses* also in the yere
1582. at an Assembly of the Empire at *Ausburgh*, by fauour
& assistance of the Spanish ministers, & of the Princes & Pre-
lats of the Romish religion (the most part whereof were at the
de-

deuotion of the house of *Austrich*)had vpon their complaints and iniurious informations obtained a Decree, for the expelling of the Trade and residence of the Merchants Aduenturers out of the Empire, and otherwise by new occasions of losses, sustained at sea by English men of warre (though nothing were done to the contrarie to the law of Nations)were so incensed, not onely against the said Merchants Aduenturers, but also against the whole English name, so that there was litle or no hope or liklihood to find any friendship, or good entertainment at their hands.

*Commissioners sent to treat with the Hamburgers of new priuiledges.*

The Companie, all these difficulties notwithstanding, taking new courage, and moued in dutie towards her Maiestie, and their Natiue Countrie, in the yeare 1587. sent their Commissioners Sir *Richard Saltonstall* Knight, at that time their Gouernour, and Doctor *Giles Fletcher*, a Ciuilian, vnto *Hambrough* with foure ships loaden with cloath, to trie the minds of that people, and whether they could procure a residence in that Towne againe (whither they were inuited by letters of the 19. of August 1586. from the Senate) The Hamburgers notwithstanding their said letters, by the instigation of the Duke of *Parma*, who at this time was wholly intentiue in a maner to the matters of England, and had inckling of a commotion doubted among the Commons there, for want of worke (the appeasing or encrease whereof much depended vpon the M.M. Aduenturers Trade, and therefore sought by all meanes to disturbe it)held themselues verie nice and coy, and hauing daily in their Counsell Doctour *Westendorp* of *Groeninghe*, sent thither by *Verdugo*, Gouernor of Westfriseland for the King of Spaine, delayed and dallied with the foresayd Commissioners, so that after much labour spent, nothing in the end was concluded: for the Hamburgers being certified by the abouesaid Doctor *Westendorp*, of the great preparation in hand, & the inuasion intēded by the king of Spaine against England, of the happie successe whereof he promised and presumed much : and of the which the Hamburghers (it shuld seeme)conceiued no smal hope, vpon euerie dayes newes either confirmed, or recalled that, which before

fore

fore hand with much a do, had beene paffed & agreed vpon
betweene them, and the Merchants Aduenturers Commiffioners, excufing this their light dealing fometime by the vn-
willingnes of their Commons(whofe confents, as they fayd,
they could not obtaine) otherwhiles, by want of authoritie
from the reft of the *Hanfes*, without whofe priuitie and liking
they might not conclude any fuch thing: and yet they had
written the contrarie in the abouefaid letter, in thefe words:
*Neque tamen ad has noftras priuatas Confultationes reliquarum
Ciuitatum Confederataru confenfum requirendum arbitramur.*
So that in fine the Commiffioners being wearied with thefe
delayes, and finding that at *Stade*, a Towne not farre diftant   *Situation of the*
from *Hambourgh*, the Trade might be wel feated, thither they   *towne of Stade.*
repaired, & procured a refidence, & Priuiledges there in the
moneth of September 1587. This town of *Stade* is an ancient
free Towne of the Empire, in the territorie of the Archbifhop
of *Breme*, who as protector of the Towne, hath a Tolle there,
but no other command. It is fituate from the riuer of *Elb* a-
bout two Englifh miles, out of the which is a creek called the
*Swinge*, which ebbeth and flow eth vp to the Towne, and is
able to carie a fhip of fourefcore or an hundred tunnes, and
maketh a fafe and quiet harbour for fhips in all weathers. The
Towne ftandeth vpon the maine land of Germanie, on the
hither fide of the Elb, a dayes iourney from *Bremen*, three
dayes iourney from *Embden*, as many from *Caffell* in *Heffen-
land*, two dayes iourney from *Lunenburgh*, and from *Hambourgh* fixe houres: verie neere and conuenient for *Weftfalia*,
*Freefland*, and the parts there abouts: in the winter feafon, and
alwayes, farre better & commodioufer then *Hambourgh*, for
tranfporting, and fending of goods to an ifro the abouefaid
Townes and parts of Dutchland. In this Towne therefore, lying fo commodious and fit for trade, though old and vnfrequented, the Company at their owne great cofts & charges,
by their aboue faid Comiffioners, obtained Priuiledges, with   *Priuiledges ob-*
the allowance and good liking of the Archbifhop & Chap-   *tained at Stade.*
ter of *Breme*: and there they found great & quicke vtterance
of their comodities at good rates & prices, Merchants refor-

G                   ting

ting thither from all parts, for in the whole Towne of *Stade*
was not one Merchant before the Companie of M.M. Aduēturers comming thither, but they liued generally all the in-
habitants thereof vpon tillage, feeding of cattell, ſwine, and
other husbandrie: the Towne alſo with the houſes and buildings thereof, was almoſt vtterly decayed, and growne rui-
nous, but in the ten yeares that the Company reſided in that
Towne, there was a ſtrange alteration, ſo that indeed it grew
to be another Towne in regard of that it was before: & as the
eſtate of *Stade* mended daily, ſo the Trade increaſed, till the
publication of the Emperours Mandate in the yeare 1597.
the end of which Mandate, a blind man may ſee to be none
other then through the ſide of the M.M. Aduenturers to hurt
and wound the ſtate of England; that is, by the ſubuerſion of
that Companie, to ſtop the vent of Engliſh Cloth, by the
which ſo manie thouſands are fed and ſuſtained in the land,
and muſt want if the Trade faile, to repoſſeſſe the *Hanſes* with
their old antiquated, and obſolete Priuiledges, no way ſuffe-
rable by the Prince or State, and to gratifie the Capitall enemies of this Realme. And therefore I could wiſh all the wel-
willers, and louers of the Common-wealth and ſtate of England, and all the good ſubiects of her Maieſtie, that through
enuie, or miſconceit they ſeeke not, or procure the decay or
hinderance of the aboueſaid Company, leaſt vnawares they
ioyne hands with the common enemie, who ſeeketh not only the ſubuerſion of the ſaid Companie, but alſo of this whole
Realme, from the which the Lord in mercie preſerue vs.

By that which hath beene aboue ſet downe, I doubt not
but it already in part appeareth, how true it is by late experience at home, that the Commoditie of the Realme can neither ſo well, nor in ſo great quantitie be vented by any other
courſe, as by maintaining the Aduenturers in their trade and
Priuiledges: for further proofe whereof, and that forreigne
wares are by this meanes brought into the land at the more
reaſonable rates, let vs ſee what hath happened abroad, and
conſider the particular doings of ſome fellowes and brethren
of the ſaid Companie.

In

In the yeare 1584. and a few yeares before, some of the *Norenbergh tra-* Companie had found out, and vsed a Trade to the Towne of *ders, and traders* *Norenberghe*, and other parts of Germanie, contrarie to the *townes.* olde good orders of the Companie, especially that which forbiddeth trade out of the Mart Townes, ordained for the keeping in credite, and better vent of English Commoditie, and bringing in of forreigne wares good cheape, & at reasonable prices. So that where the Trade was before times in the Mart Townes betweene English and forreigne Merchants, it was now growne (especially in the Towne of *Embden*) to be betweene English and English Merchants. Those which vsed this trade, to excuse their doings, alleaged, that they did transport and carie from the Mart Townes as great a quantitie of Clothes, Kersies, and other woollen commodities, and at as good prices, as the Merchant stranger did, or would doe, and that they brought to the Mart-Townes as much forreigne Ware, and that as good, and as good cheape, as the Straunger Merchantes could doe, and therefore, if the Merchants Aduenturers were not of an enuious disposition, they could be content, that their owne Countrey-men and brethren should rather gaine then straungers. Hereunto it was answered : That although all this were true, and graunted (as it was not, for that much might be excepted there againft) yet all men of sound reason and vnderstanding, might easily see and perceiue, that a Commoditie sought for at the Mart Townes, is more esteemed by the seeker thereof there, then if it were brought home, and offered him to sell at his owne doores : and the Merchants prouerbe is *(That there is twentie in the hundred difference betweene, Will you buy ? and will you sell?)* And therefore, admit that these Traders to *Norenbergh* did transport frō the Mart townes as many Clothes, Kersies, &c. as the strange Merchants did, or would do, yet could not the said Clothes, Kersies, &c. beare such price and estimation in *Norenbergh*, and other parts of Germany, being there offred to sel by English, as they wold do, if they were to be sold by strãgers, or the naturals of the place, for the aboue writtē reason: the like might be said & vnderstood of forreign

G 2                    Wares,

Wares, that the same would be bought as good cheap at the least in the Mart Townes, as they are to be bought at the Strangers owne doores: besides, it was found, that, as some sorts of silke wares were in a greater quantitie then heretofore brought by the said *Norenbergh* traders into England, so were the same wares much falsified, & empaired, in respect of their former goodnes and substance, since the beginning of the said new & disordered Trade & dealing: ouer and aboue all this, who knoweth not that the Merchants straungers are either ignorant for the most part, or haue not so perfect aduise from time to time, as the English Traders had, how English & forreigne commodities rise & fal in England? By reason whereof, there is more aduantage in selling to the said strangers, & in buying of them, then in dealing with the English *Norenberge* traders: for that they, or their friends are weekly in the Cloth-market at *London*, & so may, & no doubt do take knowledge, what price euery sort & kind of Cloth, & Kersie beareth: & then, being throughly acquainted with the Exchange, do calculate the reckening of the orderly Merchant Aduenturer, & share him such gaine as liketh them: and when they bring their forreigne Commodities to the Mart Townes, knowing before hand what is in request in England, they either sell the same at excessiue prices, or as they list themselues, or ship the into England: & often reseruing the best wares to themselues, do barter & sell the refuse in the Mart Townes: to conclude, they buy forreigne wares at *Norenberghe*, & elsewhere vpon credite, for the current answering whereof, (as is well to be prooued) they sell their English Clothes and Kersies at vile and base prices, so raising their gaines vpon forreigne wares, & casting away the commodities of the Realme: and thus the strange Merchants are put from their accustomed trade with the M.M. Aduenturers in the Mart-Towns for English commodity, & the M.M. Aduenturers fro buying of forreigne wares at the stragers hands, as much as lyeth in the said Norembergh Traders. Lastly, whereas it was sayd by them that if the M.M. Aduenturers were not of an enuious disposition, they would be content,

and

and wish that their Countreymen and brethren should rather gaine then strangers : The M. M. Aduenturers are here in wrongfully charged, for they can be very well content, to see their Countreymen, much more their brethren to thriue, and gaine, but whē as such gaine (reaching also but to a few) is much more hurtfull to the Common weale of England, and to the generall bodie of the Company of M.M. Aduenturers, then beneficiall to the said few persons, traders to *Norenberghe*, and other places out of the Marte townes, there is no reason, but that it ought to be forbidden, and cut off : for such priuate and vnwonted trade between English and English in the Marte townes, and such stragling by free, and vnfree English vsed in Germanie, and the townes of the Lowe Countries out of the Marte townes, is so vnseemely, vnmerchantlike, and farre differing from the ancient, laudable, and right English maner of the M M. Aduenturers our Predecessours in former times, & is so offensiue to all forreigne States, and people, as nothing can be more : and hath been well seen and perceiued in the *Hamburghers*, & Earle *Edgard* of *Embdē*, who were much displeased with the disordred trade at *Norenberghe* and elsewhere : saying that they had giuen the Aduenturers leaue to trade with all kinde of forreigners in their cities, but had no meaning, that their cities should bee vsed as through Faires, by trading from thence into other partes of the Empire, thereby to hinder the repaire of forreigne M. M. to the said Cities : the said Earle went further, & compelled such Englishmen as traded to *Norenberghe*, to pay Tole, not only for such clothes, kerseyes & English wares as they should transport & carry from *Embden*, but also for such forreigne wares as they brought from other partes vnto *Embden*, to the great preiudice of the State, & of the M.M. Aduenturers, who by Priuiledge were before free of all Tolles, & exactions whatsoeuer either inwards or outwards, & surely it may bee presumed, that the *Hanses* deriued that their false slunder of the Companie of M.M. Aduenturers, in charging them with *Monopolie*, from none other head nor ground then from this disordred trade vsed between a fewe vnbridled and priuate

English

English andEnglish within the Marte-townes, and without
the Marte-townes into the parts of Germànie,whereby they
shew an exorbitant,and vnsatiable desire, and greedines of
gaine, as not content with a reasonable trade in the Marte-
towne,but inchroching as it were, vpon the whole trade of
those parts,and of other men which cànnot choose, but be a
great ey-sore;and offence to all forreigne, and strange Merchants. Now,although I hope by this time it sufficiently appeareth , that the gouerned and well-ordered trade of the
M.M.Aduenturers Companie,is farre to be preferred before
a dispersed,stragling,and promiscuous trade, so that it needeth no further proofe or demonstration, yet because some
men hold this to be against the libertie of the subiect,& think
that the Aduenturers by their orders, restraine or limite the
Cloth market at home,it shal be necessarie for these mens satisfaction also, to say something further of this matter.First,
it is true that *Bonum quo communius ,eo maius:*and it were to be
wished,that there were enough for euery man, but that will
neuer be: furthermore,he looseth a piece of his libertie well,
that being restrained of a little, fareth better in that estate,
then if he were left to his owne greedy appetite: for we haue
seene by experiéce,that many men in our time leaping from
their shops and retayling,wherein they were brought vp,and
gathering great wealth,& taking vpon them to be M.M.and
dealers beyond the seas,haue in fewe yeres growne poore,or
so decayed in state that they might well haue wished, that
they had neuer left their former trade,& vocation,but suffered others quietly to enioy their priuiledge,and disgested the
losse of a litle scrap of liberty,hurtfull to themselues & rightly
bestowed vpon others for such seruices,deserts,& considera-
tions,as no other subiect need to enuy them for the same, or
to be agreeued thereat,except they wil chalége the Prince of
partiality, or not to haue a due care of the subiect, or say that
the preferment or exemption, which one mà hath more,and
before another in the Common wealth,is against the libertie
of the subiect,& so bring in an ilfaueured confusion, or into-
lerable equality,by vsurping vpon other mens rights.& patri-
mony

mony ſo dearely obtained, and with their great and exceſſiue
charges and trauel, maintained certaine hundred yeres together, as the Freedom which the Company of M.M. Aduenturers inioyeth, hath been. But (I pray you) let vs ſee what
would follow, if theſe men had that which they ſo much deſire & contend for, ſurely nothing els then that which hitherto we haue ſeene to haue failen out : neither can there any
better end come thereof, then heretofore of the like. For example : The Engliſh had at the *Narue* in *Liefland*, a profitable
trade, and good ſales for their Countrey commoditie a good
while together, till at length in the yere 1565. a number of
ſtragling Marchants reſorting thither out of this Realme, the
trade was vtterly ſpoiled, inſomuch that many of them went
about the towne with cloth vpon their armes, and meaſures
in their hands, and ſold the ſame by the *Arſine*, a meaſure of
that Countrey, to the great inbaſing of that excellent Commoditie, the diſcredite of our Nation, and the finall impoue-
riſhing, and vndoing of many of the ſaid ſtraglers, which
being made knowne to her Maieſtie, and her Highneſ right
Honourable priuie Counſell, order was taken at the next
Parliament, that the Towne of *Narue* ſhould be compriz.ed
within the Charter of the *Muſcouie* Company, to preuent
the like pedlarlike kinde of dealing euer after, & the making
vile of the principalleſt commodity of the realme. Which one
example among other, may ſerue for verificatió of that which
heretofore hath bene ſaid againſt the ſtragling & ſingle Merchants trade in Woollen com̄nodity, wherin further may be
noted that which by experience is found true, that in the vn-
gouerned ſingle trade, the firſt commer marreth the Market
for him that commeth after, and at his reiurne maketh haſte
(as his maner is) to preuent thoſe which follow, he ſetteth vp
his wares at a high price, which afterwards are hardly pulled
downe to a lower rate: the which is otherwiſe in the gouerned
trade of the M.M. Aduenturers: for comming together, and
at one inſtant to market, or their Mart-Towne, where they
are priuiledged with códitions & exemptiós to their owne liking, & for the furtherance of the Commerce, ſufficient order

*The pedlarlike
dealing of the
Engliſh ſtraglers
at the Narue.*

is

is taken for the preuenting one of another, & keeping in estimation of the commoditie of the land without vsing any such indirect dealing, for this purpose as the *Hanses* haue falsely imagined & as impudetly published, wheras the single & stragling trader, wanting all the abouesaid helps & means, lyeth open to sundry wrongs, inconeniences, & grieuaces which to strangers are incident & comon in strange places, & thereby are made subiect to many exactios, new tolles, & excessiue payments & charges for one cause or other, & consequently as soone impouerished & driuen from their trade by the forreign Merchants, or after they haue made the forreign M.M. acquainted with the trade, are eaten out by them: which also would happen to the M.M. Aduenturers, if the M.M. Aduenturers, if they were not so vnited, and held together by their good gouernmet, & by their politike, & merchantlike orders.

Here it may be obiected, that the more buyers there are, the quicker sales, & higher prices, and therefore of all others, as well of the M.M. Aduenturers might transport Cloth, the more would be sold, & the prices would be the higher: To this I haue sufficiently answered before & prooued the contrary by experience fetched from the twenty ninth yeere of her Maiesties reigne, when as all, both English and strangers, that would, were by letters Pattents directed from her Highnesse to the Lord Treasurers, enabled to buye and transport English cloth, & for that the Charter of the citie of *London* should not bee in the way, or an hindrance hereunto (by reason that vnfree men are thereby restrained from buying and selling within the said citie, and that the ordinarie Market-place at that time for Cloth was in Blackwell-hall) the signe of the *George* at *Westminster* in the Kings-street was appointed a market-place, for such Clothiers to resort vnto as would take the libertie of the aforesaid Letters patentes, but what folowed thereof? I could neuer yet learne, that one Wayne load of Cloth was vnloaded at the saide place, neither that the Steelyard Merchants nor any of her Maiesties subiects so erabled as aforesaid, did euer take benefit by the same for fourtie clothes, one man yet liuing only excepted, who since (as I

haue

heard)hath often protested, that in buying 200. Clothes, he
lost a good summe of his principall, and no maruaile, seeing
those who had serued and had beene brought vp in the trade
of a Marchant Aduenturer many yeers together, could hardly make one of one, such was the longsomenes of Returne,
and the badnes of the time at that instant, through the Con-
iunction of many difficulties not here inserted, besides those
which haue beene aboue touched. So that not the want of
buyers was the cause of the complaint of want of worke, and
trade at that time, but rather the abouesaid causes. For it is
very well knowne, that the Company of M. M. Aduenturers
is sufficient and able enough, and ouer many to buy vp, and
vent all that Cloth, and those sortes of woollen commoditie,
made and endraped within the Realme, wherewith they vsu-
ally deale, and which are vendible in the Countries, whither
they trade beyond the seas: for they are not so fewe as 3500.
personsin number enhabiting London, & sundry Cities and
partes of the realme, especially the townes that lye conueni-
ently for the sea, of which a very great many vse not the trade
for that it sufficeth for al, but are constrained to get their liuing
by some other meanes: and to the the end that those which
are traders may be equally and indifferently cared and soried
for, and that the wealthie or richer sort with their great purses
may not engrosse the whole Commoditie into their owne
hands, and so some haue all, and some neuer a whit, there is a
stint, and reasonable proportion allotted, and set by an ancient order & manner, what quantitie either at once, or by the
yere euery man may ship out or transport, which he is not to
goe beyond nor exceed: which whole stint and proportion,
if it were shipped or transported out of the lande, would a-
mount vnto y erely the double quãtitie of al the cloth of those
sorts made in the Realme, which the Merchants Aduenturers
deale in, wherby it is euident that this stinting is not a restraint
or limitation of the Cloth marked (as some of late haue mis-
conceiued) but rather an œconomicall, and discreet partiti-
on, or ap(propor)ioning among the members, and Brethren of
the Company, of the commodities, and benefits of the same:

*3500. Freemen of the Company of M.M. Aduenturers.*

H                                             so

so that the wealthier sort are not forgotté, but withal are kept from engroſſing the whole trade, contrarie to the vſe and maner of a well ordered Common wealth, or family, wherein all are prouided for, and not ſome ſtarued for want, whileſt others are ſwollen vp to the eyes with fat and plentie : *For it is merry in Hall, where beards wagge all,* according to that olde right Engliſh Prouerbe of our Anceſtours, who full well vnderſtood what belonged to good houſe keeping, and practiſed the ſame better then in theſe our dayes is vſed, the more the pittie.

---

*That the Nauigation of the Realme, is maintained and aduanced by the Companie of the M.M. Aduenturers.*

 INCE the erection of the Company of M.M. Aduenturers, and of other Companies trading *Ruſſia, Eaſtland, Spaine, Turkie, &c.* the Nauigation of the Realme is merueilouſly increaſed in number of good ſhipping, and of able, and skilfull maſters & Mariners, in ſo much that whereas within theſe 60. yeeres, there were not aboue foure ſhips, beſides thoſe of her Maieſties Nauie Royal, about the burthen of 120 Tunnes, within the Riuer of *Thames,* there are now at this day to be found pertaining to *London,* and other places lying vpon the ſaid Riuer a great number of very large and ſeruiceable Marchants ſhips, fit as well for the defence of the Realme (if need were) as for traffick, whereof a good part are ſet on worke by the ſaid Companie of M.M. Aduenturers : the reaſon whereof is, that this, and other Companies tranſporting at once or at one inſtant, a great quantitie of goods and wares, and being to make returne of the ſame in forreign commodities, do go in fleets, or with great & warlike veſſels well furniſhed, & this maner of going in fleet to the Marte-Towne tendeth to the ſafety and pre-

preseruation of the shipping, and goods of the subiects of the
Realme, which amount to a great valew, and would help the
enemie, and hurt our State very much, if it should come into
his handes, being thereby able to defend themselues from
spoyle and violence, so that since the troubles beganne with
Spaine, not one ship set out by the Companie of M.M. Aduenturers hath beene taken by the enemie, whereas the single Merchant going where, and when he listeth, and not able
to set a good ship on worke, casteth howe to come of good
cheape, and either shippeth in strangers, or prouideth himselfe of small vessels and Pinkes, to serue his turne for small
quantities of wares, and fit to flie, or run away if hee should
chance to meet with the enemie, and yet hee is many times
snapped vp and made a praye to Dunkerkers, and other Sea-
rouers, both to his owne, and the publike hurt, as we haue often times knowne of late yeres, wherby it appeareth that the
Nauigation of the Realme is maintained, aduanced, and
encreased by the vpholding of the Company of M.M. Aduenturers, and of the later Companies also.

---

## That the *Queenes Customes* and *Incomes*, are augmented by maintaining the Companie of M.M. *Aduenturers.*

THE like reason is for the increasing of her
Maiesties Customes, and Incomes, as is
for the Nauigation : for if the good and
seruiceable shipping of this Realme bee
mainetained, bettered and increased
by the great Trade and Trafficke of the
sayde Companie, and if that greater quantities of Cloth are
transported and vttered by them in forreigne partes, then if
all were free and set at large, as hath beene aboue plainely
and throughly proued, it followeth necessarily that their said
vnited trade is more aduantageable, and yeeldeth more ample and certaine profite, and encrease to her Highnesse Customes, then a single, stragling, or loose trade by any meanes

can

can doe : The Cuſtome alſo which the ſaid Company pay-
eth, commeth in yerely, & at certaine times in round ſummes
and payments, wherby the turne of the Prince, and State is
the better ſerued vpon any occaſion of need of money: wheras the payments of the ſingle Merchants come in by driblets,
and ſmall parcels : and hereunto the good orders of the
ſayd Companie, are no ſmall helpe, eſpecially in tranſportati-
on, or ſhipping outwardes, for that the moſt part of the Commodities, which the Marchants Aduenturers carry out of the
Realme, being ſhipped in appointed ſhippes at *London*, the
ſaid Company haue their certaine ouerſeers, by whoſe order,
and appointment they ſhip that which they ſhip, and when
the goods ariue on the other ſide of the Seas, there are alſo
officers who attend, and take view of the Packs, Fardels, and
other parcels of Commoditie landed, preſenting, and en-
forming of ſuch, which they finde to haue ſhipped in other
maner then was appointed them to ſhip, or not to haue entred and payd their Cuſtome and dueties rightly to her Maieſtie, who are ſubieĉt to great penalties, and forfeitures for
the ſame : this courſe deuiſed for the better collecĉtion of an
Impoſition leuied by the Company vpon Cloth and other
things for the maintenance, and vpholding of the ſaid Company, doeth not onely the better make knowen vnto them,
but alſo vnto her Highneſſe Officers of the Cuſtome-houſe,
what euery man ſhippeth away, ſo that by this meanes the
Cuſtome is the truelier, and fuller payed, whereas the ſtragler ſhipping his Cloth and other Commoditie in couert maner, hugger-mugger, and at obſcure Portes, haue more
aduantage, and meanes to defraude her Maieſtie of her dueties and rightes, then thoſe which ſhip at *London*, and other
great Port Townes, either by falſe entryes, colouring of
Straungers goods, and corrupting the Cuſtomers, and o-
ther Officers, who, for the moſt part being needie perſons in
thoſe ſmall, and remote Portes of the Realme, are more readie to take rewardes, and cloſelier may doe it, then the Officers of the Cuſtomes at the Port of *London* : to ſay nothing of
the great quantity of forreign wares brought into the realme
by

by the Merchants Aduenturers, the Cuſtome whereof is better, and trulier paid, then if the ſtragler, or ſtranger had the
importation or paiment thereof, or of the like quantitie, and
if the Records were ſearched, no doubt, but it would ſo bee
found. For it was not without ſome cauſe, that heretofore we
haue ſeene ſo great fraternitie, familiaritie, kindneſſe, and in-
warde friendſhip betweene the Officers for her Maieſties
Cuſtomes, and ſtrangers, and that the ſaid Officers aboue all
others, now wiſh them againe ſo heartily, and call ſo loud for
them, as though now the State were dangerouſly diuided, &
vnkindly at iarre with her ancient allies, and beſt forreigne
friends, and therefore time to prouide againſt a deſolation,
which the land is ready to fall into ( for want of theſe deare
Allies, and kind friends forſooth) whileſt no man is found, that
layeth it to heart, and bringeth them in againe. Surely this is
well preached for ſtockfiſh and Rheniſh wine &c. The Alderman of the Steelyard, & *Emanuel van Meteren* haue great
cauſe to giue them thanks, but not her Maieſtie, or the State :
the reaſons I haue ſufficiently laid open, and ſhewed in this
Diſcourſe, whereunto I referre the indifferent and diſcreete
Reader. As for thoſe Strangers, who haue termed the Companie of Merchants Aduenturers, *A Priuate, Particular, and
Preuenting Company,* or haue written, or foreſpoken in that
ſort of the ſaide Company, if it be ſo, as theſe Cuſtomers ſay,
they haue thereby well ſhewed their skill in P.P. & that they
are not onely ſtrangers to our ſtate and common wealth, but
withall priuie vnderminers, and maligners of the good therof : and let theſe Cuſtomers, while they warne other men,
be wiſe, and warned themſelues alſo, leaſt by their too too
much leaning vnto, and fauouring of ſuch ſtraungers, they
proue not in the end bad Cuſtomers to her Maieſtie, and conſequently, corrupt and vnnaturall members of their Countrie
and State : & withall let them vnderſtand and be well aſſured
that the Merchants Aduenturers both know, and regard the
eſſentiall parts, grounds and pillers of Traffike, & of old time
haue put them in practiſe, and yet at this day do quietlier, better, and certainlier obſerue & maintaine them, then the Cu-

*Cuſtomers of the out Ports backe-bite the M.M. Aduenturers.*

ftomers of the out-ports (I feare me) do their office: Laftly,
where they fay, that the M.M.Aduenturers by a bare and idle
pretence of the word *Order*, and orderly tranfporting of the
Credite and Creame of the Land *(Cloth)* haue brought the
trade thereof to a kinde of confufion, and themfelues into
fuch a Labyrinth, that befides the diftreffe of the Clothiers,
with all their dependents, and generall complaints at home
(to their honorable Lordfhips endleffe offence, and trouble
at the Councell table) the Commoditie it felfe is empaired,
abafed, and in a fort defpifed, &c. Surely, either their intelligence hath deceiued them, or they fhew themfelues to bee
caried with a malicious fpirit : for who knoweth not, that the
Trade of the Merchants Aduenturers is not in a bare or idle
pretence & fhew, but in very deed the moft orderly and beft
framed Trade that may be? True it is, that fome ftrangers and
others (poffibly of thefe Cuftomers familiars & friends) haue
by open, and couert means at home and abroad endeuoured
and done their beft to bring the faid Trade to fome notable
confufion, and thofe of the Companie into a labyrinth, to the
empairing and embafing indeed of the Commoditie of the
land : but, thanks be to God, and our alwayes gracious Ladie
Queene, they haue not yet had their wils, neither fhall they
(I hope) though thefe od Cuftomers tooke part with the neuer fo much : and therefore they may well hold their clacke,
and be content, like fubiects, with that, which thofe in high-
eft authoritie haue fo long found good, & decreed, fhall be fo
in their wifedomes, and not take vpon them like controllers,
to checke the doings, which either of ignorance they vnderftand not the ground, and reafon of, or through malice or vnnaturall affection towards ftrangers more, then their owne
Country-men, doe mifconceiue, and mifreport of : but becaufe I haue often made mention of the *Hanfes* in this Dif-
courfe, it fhall not by the way be amiffe, to fhew what thefe
*Hanfes* are, and what hath paffed betweene this State & them
in mans memorie.

 The *Hanfes* or Eafterlings, as they are commonly called,
are people of certaine free townes in Dutchland, either lying
vpon

vpon the sea,or some nauigable riuers:and were in old time
two and seuentie in number, as they say : whereof *Lubecke* of
the Wendish, *Brunswick* of the Saxon, *Dantzick* of the Prusse
and *Cullen* since it was of late yeeres receiued into this confederacie of the Westfalish Townes(for into these foure parts
or names they are diuided)were,and are the chiefest. These
Townes, by reason of their situation, and to put a distinction
betweene them and other free Townes of the Empire,were
in old time called in Dutch *Aen zee steden*,or Townes on the
sea-side,or for breuities sake *Ansesche*,or *Hansesche steden*,and
in our language *Hanse stedes*, or *Hanse townes*. These Townes
hauing vnited themselues for the sea-trade and commerce,
were full of good and great shipping, and had an exceeding
great trade and traffike in all the East countrie wares & commodities, to wit, Corne, Stockefish,Waxe, Hempe, Steele,
Masts,Firre-poles,Dele-boords,pitch,Tarre, Sopeashes,&c.
seruing diuers lads & places therwithal,& with their shipping
in time of need, by meanes whereof they got vnto themselues
large Priuiledges and immunities,to their great benefite,ad-
uantage, and enriching, and in our time they had their houses or places of residence in this realme at *London*,in Norway
at *Berghen*,in Russia at *Nouogrode*,and in the lowe Countries
at *Antwerpe*,  whither they remoued from *Bridges*: each of
these Houses had their Chiefe or Alderman, and Assistants,
with a Secretarie, Treasurer, Steward, and other necessarie
officers,but all of them held correspondence with the Town
of *Lubeck*, as head of all the *Hanse* Townes. These Aldermen
and Assistants had power to exercise Merchants law among
themselues in their house at *London*, called the *Steelyard*, so
named,by reason of the Steele, which they in great quantitie
brought thither to sell,and is a verie large and spacious house,
lying vpon the Thamis side,for that they were enioyned to
dwell all in one house. Among other their Priuiledges in England,one was,That they might carie out, and bring in their
Wares and Merchandise for an old Custome of one and a
quarter vpon the hundred, & thereby were exempt from all
personall or reall charge or contribution , which all other
Mer-

Merchants are fubiect vnto, faue that in time of neede, they were enioyned to repaire, and helpe to keep one of the gates of *London*, called *Bifhopsgate*. Now in King *Edward* the thirds time, Wooll was the beft Merchandife of this land, and the cuftome thereof the chiefeft income which the Prince receiued, as amounting yearely to the fumme of 65. or 70. thoufand pounds: which was much in thofe dayes. And we reade that in the yeare 1355. there was granted by a Parliament to king *Edward* the third, Fiftie fhillings vpon each fack of wooll to be caried out of the Realme in fixe yeares, fo that the faid King might difpend euerie day one hundred Markes, which in fixe yeares time, amounted to fifteen hundred thoufand pounds, reckoning for an hundred thoufand fackes of Wooll a yeere tranfported, fiftie fhillings vpon each facke: This woolle was for the moft part vented in the low Countries, and there wrought and endraped into Cloth: but in proceffe of time the Drapery and Art of making of Cloth was brought into this realme, and the *Hanfes*, who before time bought all their Cloth in the low Countries, and fo caried them vpwards, did now buy much Cloth in England, and tranfported the fame continually vpon the old fmall Cuftom, which at the firft was fet fo low, for the furtherance of the new begun Draperie, and Arte of making of Cloth, but at length it being growne verie great, and the Wooll trade almoft wholy decayed, it was found that the Prince and ftate loft exceedingly, by the paffing out of Cloth vpon the fayd fmall Cuftome, and therefore in Queene *Maries* dayes, after her mariage with King *Philip*, in the yeare 1557. and by his meanes the Cuftome of Cloth, Kerfie, and other Woollen Commoditie, befides forreigne wares, was raifed from 14. pence to fix fhillings 8. pence the Cloth, to be payed by Englifhmen, and 13. fhillings & foure pence by ftrangers, tranfporting the fame; by means whereof the cuftome of cloth endraped within the land, was brought to bee equall with the cuftome of Wooll, when it was moft, & when the faid wooll was caried out vnwrought, and was draped in the low Countries. Againft this the *Hanfes* oppofed themfelues, pretending

their

their priuiledges so long agoe graunted, and by many Kings
confirmed vnto them, as they said, but for that in the yeare
1550. vnder King *Edward* the sixth, vpon due examination
of their pretended Priuiledges, there were many defects and
faults found therein, and for that the *Hanses* for diuers abuses,
and falshoods in colouring, and freeing of forreigne goods, or
such, which ought not to enioy the libertie of the *Hanses*, being none of their vnion or confederacie, and for other causes,
had beene by a Decree of the Councell adiudged to be fallen from their said Priuiledges, part whereof were presently
resumed & called in, especially that which concerned the carying out of Woollen Cloth: they obtained no remedy all
that Kings dayes, but since they haue beene offered great fauour, as by that which followeth shall appeare. But not content herewithall, they made their often cōplaints to the Emperours Maiesty, of the wrong done them, in seazing of their
Priuiledges in England. First, in the yeare 1564. at which
time the English Cloth was banished out of the Low Countries by the Dutchesse of *Parma*, for the causes heretofore ex-
pressed in this Treatise, & that the M. M. Aduenturers helde
their Marts at *Embden*: and afterwards in the yeare 1582. at an
Assembly of the Empire at *Ausburge*, charging the said Merchants Aduenturers, that they had taken away the said *Hanses* priuiledges in England, to the end, that they might haue
the whole Cloth trade in their owne hands, and so by their
Monopolish dealings make Cloth deare in the Empire : setting also price before hand of that which they sell, and of that
which they will buy, and so committing open Monopoly.
Whereupon the Emperour wrote vnto the Earle of *Embden*,
commaunding him to banish the M. M. Aduenturers out of
his Countrie, as Monopolish persons, and hurtfull to the Empire. The Earle discreetly considering that her Maiestie
might, and could easily answer the slanderous complaints of
the *Hanses*, charging her Highnesse with wrong done vnto
them, as she did, by her letters sent to the Emperour in Aprill
1581. by M. *George Gilpin*, at that time Secretarie to the Company: & that the said M. M. Aduēturers were now in his town

*Some of the Han-
ses calumniation
against the M.
Aduenturers*

I of

of *Embden* no more to be accounted Monopolians, then they
were heretofore in *Antwerp*, and of late at *Hamburgh*, during
their refidence there ten yeeres together, & vpwards, did not
only not put the faid Decree or Commandement of the Emperour in execution, but tooke vpon him by his Orator at
*Spieres*, to defend the Trade of the M. M. Aduenturers in the
Empire, and to iuftifie the entertainment of the into his countrie, wherein Doctor *William Muller*, at that time Chancellor
to the faid Earle, and fince *Sindicus* of *Hamburgh*, was a chiefe
Counfellor or actor: fo that the Emperour, for that time, was
well fatisfied with the Earles doings and anfwer: and the faid
M.M. Aducturers continued their trade at *Embden*, till that by
the D. of *Parmaes* too neere and bad neighbourhood, and o-
ther vrgent caufes, they were forced of neceffitie, & for the
better vent of the commodity of the Realme, to feeke for a
new place, and finally, to agree with the *Staders*, as is aboue
at large rehearfed: howbeit the *Hanfes* here ceafed not, but
perfifted in their former purfuits & Complaints, till the yeare
1597. at which time the faid *Hanfes* were much endamma-
ged at fea by Englifhmen of warre, who by vertue of a Proclamation fet forth by her Maieftie, tooke many fhips of the
Eafterlings going into Spaine with corn, ammunition, & furniture for fhipping, all which was made good bootie & prize;
which doing caufed the *Hanfes* to haue the better audience
in their complaints, the yeare before by *Don Francefco de
Mendoza*, Admiral of Arragon, in the name of the K. of Spain:
and the Archduke *Albert* highly recommended to the Emperour, & earneftly follicited vnder pretext of withftanding,
and chaftifing of Pirates and fea-robbers: to the forwarding
of this bufineffe holpe not a little, that in May and Iune 1597.
*Florence* Earle of *Barlamont*, Doctor *George Weftendorpe*, and
*Iohn van Nickercken*, Counfellors, were fent vnto the King of
*Denmarke*, & to the *Hanfe* Towns, & namely to the Town of
*Lubecke*, on the behalf of the King of Spaine, & the Archduke
*Albert*. Thefe Embaffadours comming to the faid Towne of
*Lubecke*, did in writing declare the ancient friedfhip betweene
the houfe of *Burgundie*, and the *Hanfe* Townes, & how much
the

the said king had aduanced & recommēded their cause vnto the Emperour, touching their Priuiledges in England, by the means of his Embaſſadour *Don Guillame de S. Clement*, reſident at *Praghe*: They alſo complained, that the *Hanſe* townes vſed ſo ample trade with the kings rebels (as they termed thē) the low Countries, by means whereof the Queene of Englād was the more emboldened, & ſtrengthened againſt the ſaid King, wherefore they required, that the *Hanſe* townes would for a time forbeare all trade whatſoeuer with the ſaid rebels, that therby they might the ſooner be reduced vnder their K. obediēce: but if they feared to do this, by reaſon of the league betweene England, France, & the States of the vnited Prouinces, then they required, that they would alſo deale & traffique with the kings true and loyall ſubiects in the Hauens of *Callice, Grauelingh, Dunkercke, Nieuport Sluyſe*, & *Antwerp*, as well as they did with the Hollanders, otherwiſe their trade might be well accounted for Partialitie, rather then Neutralitie; promiſing further, that the ſaid *Hanſes* ſhould diſcharge their goods, buy, ſell, and make returne in the forſaid Hauens, without any paiment at all of Toll Impoſt, Licenſe, or other charge whatſoeuer; and further, ſhould be aſſured, and warranted by the Archduke *Albert*, from all dammage or loſſe. Theſe Embaſſadors alſo ſeemed to be much grieued for the iniurie, which they ſaid the Queene of England did vnto the *Hanſes*, in taking from them their ſo ancient Priuiledges, for the recouerie whereof they offered all poſſible aſſiſtance, and to receiue them vnder the Kings protection: moreouer, to furniſh them with ſhips, munition, money, and ſouldiors at all times, as need ſhuld require: offering them beſides free trade and traffike in Spaine & Portingall, ſo that they ſeparated & diſtinguiſhed their ſhips frō thoſe of the kings rebellious ſubiects by ſome marke or token, as they ſhould think beſt. Laſtly they ſhewed, that the King had giuen order to the Archduke *Albert*, to ſend a notable Embaſſage to the Emperour to procure the ſetting forth of the Mandat or Decree agreed vpō at *Ausburgh* 1582. againſt the Monopoliſh Engliſh trade (as they pleaſed to cal it) thereby to effect the reſtitutiō of the

*Hanses* Priuiledges,& that his disobediēt subiects,the Queen
of England,& the King of Nauarre,as disturbers of the peace
of Christendome,and stirters vp of the Turke, might once be
suppressed,destroied,& rewarded according to their deserts.
And albeit since the troubles of the low Countries, the *Hanses* haue beene shewed but small fauour,the said Embassadors
requested notwithstanding that they would helpe to further
the Embassage, which the King of Denmarke had promised
to send vnto the Queen of England, king of Nauarre,and the
rebellious States, and to compell them to right and reason,
which the King of Spaine & the Archduke should at all times
acknowledge for a singular pleasure. About this time also the
Kings of Denmarke,and Polone, the Emperour, & the Princes of the Empire sent their Embassadours into England, and
vnto the States of the vnited low Countries, all which was
procured and brought to passe by the King of Spaine and his
Ministers,to none other end, but to make the English as Pirates and robbers at sea, and the Netherlanders, as rebels a-
gainst their Prince,hated & odious vnto all the world, taking
vpon them also the cause of the said *Hanses* lost Priuiledges,
which they pretend to haue in England, as by intercepted
letters was sufficiently made knowne and manifested to the
Queens Maiesty & the states of the vnited low Countries.

The King of Polones Embassador *Paul d'Ialine*, had audience of her Maiestie the 4th of August 1597. who in strange
and vnlooked for maner & termes, declared vnto her Highnesse,that the subiects of the King his Maister *Sigismond* the
third,were not only not gratified with anie new benefite, or
fauor at her Maties hands,but to the cotrarie were depriued of
commodities & freedomes which her predecessours had giuen and confirmed vnto them, and consequently were de-
barred of all trade and traffique in her kingdome. That likewise her Maiestie had set forth certaine Edicts or Proclamations, by the which,contrarie to the law of Nations, the Na-
uigations, and trade into Spaine was forbidden, and vnder
colour thereof diuerse ships of the subiects of the said King
had beene taken at sea, and the goods therein made prize,
and

and confiscate, whereof he required reparation, & reſtitution, and that the trade Weſtward might remain free and open to thoſe of *Polone*, otherwiſe his maſter the King ſhould be forced to vſe ſuch meanes as thereby neighbourly freedom and reſtitution might be obteined. This was in briefe the effect of the ſaide Embaſſadours ſpeech, which with a very loude voice he deliuered in the Latine tongue: Whereunto it pleaſed her Maieſtie to make him a ſhort anſwere, and quicke for that time, referring him for further anſwere to certaine of her Highneſſe Honourable priuie Counſell, to wit, the Lorde *Burghley*, late high Treaſurer deceaſed, the Lord high Admiral, Sir *Iohn Forteſcue*, and Sir *Robert Cecill* Secretarie: to whom after the ſaid Poliſh Embaſſadour had deliuered his ſpeech, which hee made before the Queene in writing, and excuſed his rough kinde of ſpeaking, ſhewing that by his Commiſſion ſigned, and ſealed by the King in the aſſembly of the States of *Polone* he was thereunto enioyned, he receiued the anſwere following in the name of her Maieſtie, which properly pertaining to the matter of the *Hanſes*, and anſwering fully, and very pertinently the queſtion made by them about their old priuiledges, I haue thought meete to inſert in this place.

THE ſaid Honourable Perſonages therefore told him, that her Maieſtie, vnderſtanding of his comming into *England*, was right glad thereof, as ſent from the king her brother, for whom not long ſince ſhe had by her Interceſſion obtained, Firſt a Truce, and afterwardes a peace of the great Turke, when the ſaid King and his State was oppreſſed with ſore warre, which peace he yet inioyeth to the great good, and benefite of his Kingdome, and therefore now expected, not onely a remembrance of the ſaid good turne, but alſo due thanks for the ſame, for that neuer ſince ſhe had receiued any from him: her Highneſſe had giuen him gracious audience, and read the King his maſters Letters willingly, wherin ſhee ſawe nothing but that which ought to proceed *A Rege fratre*, ad *Reginam ſororem Chariſſimam*, but ſay they, you

*Anſwere made on her Maieſties behalfe vnto the Embaſſage.*

I 3 change-

ing as it should seeme the person of an Ambassadour, began
a long speach, and turned the same almost into a sermone,
the which notwithstanding her Maiesty heard with patience,
signifying vnto you onely in a fewe wordes, beseeming the
Maiestie of a Prince, howe vnworthily you in your Oration
had laid the fault of many things vpon her Highnes, and with
how great equitie in deede she hoped that her actions would
be well liked of all men, and so dismissed you to receiue further answere according to your negotiation of vs her Counsellours, who are best witnesses of all her doings almost these
fourtie yeere, as well with the kings her friends, as with her e-
nemies, although wee know no Prince in Christendom for e-
nemie, but the king of Spaine onely,  whose cause you very
seriously handled in your speach. First therefore we required
to see your Oration in writing, to the end that we might giue
such answere thereunto, as were conuenient, and for that you
haue shewed vnto vs your commission sealed and signed by
the king of *Polone* (as appeared vnto vs) in the assembly of
that kingdom, whereby we haue plainely perceiued, that you
haue vttered nothing in your Oration, which you had not order to declare, therefore we can in no wise blame you for any
thing by you said, although her Maiestie looked not for any
such matter. Concerning the points of your complaintes, we
obserue them to be these: First you say, that your king percei-
ueth that his subiects haue not onely not receiued any newe
benefite from her Maiestie, but are partly depriued of those,
proceeded fró her Highnes progenitors, and were confirmed
vnto them, and partly are in a maner excluded from all Nauigation, or trade in this Realme: The second point, conteineth
a grieuous complaint of your kings subiects against the Proclamations sent vnto them, by the which all trafficke into
Spaine is forbidden them, and consequently that their ships
haue bene in hostile maner taken by the QVEENES men of
warre, and the goods therein made prize and confiscated, and
finally you required in the Kings name restitution of the said
goods, or reparation of the damages & iniuries (as they terme
them) receiued, as that they be not hereafter hindred in the a-
fore-

forefaid trafficke, which by the common law ought to be free
to all men, otherwife fuch meanes of neceffitie muft bee
vfed, whereby they may get fatisfaction by the aid and helpe
of the faid king: thefe beeing the chiefe heades, or pointes of
your Ambaffage, and of that which your king requireth, her
Maieftie hath thought good to anfwere thereunto fincerely,
and according to the trueth of the matter in this maner: Firft,
that your king is not rightly enformed concerning the firft
point, in that it is faid that his fubiects are partly depriued of
their Priuiledges, and partly fhut out from all Trade almoft in
this Realme: for where there is mention made of his fubiects,
as fubiects of the king of *Polone,* this doubt may arife, what
kinde of people the fubiects are, becaufe they muft be vnderftood either to bee fubiects of the Dukedome of *Pruffia,* or
elfe to bee comprifed vnder the name of the *Hanfes,* who
haue no certaine feate or place whence they are: For other
then the fubiectes of the Dukedome of *Pruffia,* and the
*Hanfes,* as Merchantes of Germanie refiding at *London,*
the QVEENES MAIESTIE neuer vnderftood, that there
were any that pretended any Priuiledge of Commerce a-
boue or before other Marchantes of all EVROPE: And
whereas they complaine as Subiectes of the King of *Polone,* that they are depriued of their Priuiledges, and almoft excluded from all Trade in this Kingdome: Firft,
concerning the right of their Priuiledges, queftion was
made almoft 50 yeres agoe in the time of King EDVVARD
the fixth of the validitie of their former Priuiledges, and then
the fayde Priuiledges were rightly iudgged voyde, and
forfeited for the manifeft breach of the Conditions thereof, and fince the fayde *Hanfes* could neuer prooue, that
they had iniurie done them in the fayde reuocation: not-
wirhftanding all this they had granted vnto them in their
Trade into this Realme, and in the payement of their
Cuftomes more libertie, then any Marchantes of what-
foeuer Nations through all EVROPE, yea by efpeciall
grace, and fauour they were made equall, and had as much
freedome giuen in their Trade, and in the payement of the
Cuftomes

Cuſtomes of their Merchandiſes, as the naturall borne Subiects of this Realme, according to the true meaning and intent of their priuiledges from the beginning: and if they haue
not accepted of this, which by great fauour was offered vnto
them, and ſo haue forborne their Trade in this Realme, the
fault is in themſelues, neither can it be rightly ſaide, that they
are excluded (as it ſhould ſeeme by the Kings writing that he
is informed) but rather admitted and retained with the ſame
fauour, as the very meere ſubiects and naturals of the Crown
of Englande are, then the which what can bee greater?
Vnleſſe, contrary to all humane Lawe, the Queene ſhould
haue more care of them, then of her proper ſubiects and how
abſurd, yea how deteſtable this ſhold be, wil be made mani-
feſt, if it be cóſidered what the office of a good prince is in the
rule; & adminiſtration of all his kingdome: for if in regard of
his kingly office a King bee compared to the husband of an
houſe, or to the Paſtor of the people, or (as he is ſaid to bee in
the diuine Scriptures) to a foſter father of the people committed vnto him, who except he were ſtarke mad, would call that
Prince a good father or husband of the houſe, which ſhould
haue more care of an other mans familie then of his own? Or
a good Paſtor or ſhephard, which neglecting his owne flock
ſhould looke better to another mans then his owne, or worthy of the name of a Nurſing or foſter King, which ſhould
neglect his owne children, and nouriſh other mens children
with his milke? And ſo theſe things may be well applyed to
the preſent cauſe and queſtion in hand: for if the *Hanſes* ſhould
haue better conditions, then the proper ſubiects of the kingdome, it would plainely follow that the Prince of this realme
ſhold do his natural ſubiects very great iniurie, cótrary to the
law of nature & mans la w, for by this means his ſubiects ſhold
become poore, or rather deſtitute of all honeſt and profitable
trafficke and Nauigation, and the *Hanſes* ſhould growe opu-
lent, and poſſeſſe the whole trade of the realme, as Monopo-
liſts of the whole kingdom. And by theſe reaſons, well waighed, it manifeſtly appeareth, that thoſe whom the king calleth
his ſubiects doe moſt falſely complaine that they are excluded

de'd from lawfull trade in this land, when as freely they may trade, and with the fame conditions as her Maiefties meere Englifh Subie&tes may doe, and with far better then all other Merchants, In fomuch as that they are preferred before all the neighbour people of this Realme, *French, Scots, Flemings, Hollanders,* and the reft of the Low Countrey Merchants, and before all the people of Dutchland, the faid *Hanfes* onely excepted. Wherefore her Maie.ftie is perfwaded, that when the king of *Polone* fhall vnderftand thefe reafons, he will change his opinion, the like fhe expe&teth at the hands of the Senatours of that Kingdome, if thefe things bee aright imparted vnto them: For the complaints of the *Hanfes* are fo vniuft, and vnreafonable, that it may be doubted, whether the accuftomed forme of iudgement in matters of doubt were obferued by the abouefaide Affembly in this caufe, or that credite was giuen to the complainants the matter but flightly examined, or that place was giuen to their importunate prayers and requefts: For her Maiefty hath that opinion of the fupreme authority, and dexteritie of the Senatours of *Polone* in their proceedings, in the Affemblies of the faide Kingdome (which commeth not to the King by inheritance, but by ele&tion, and confent of the faid Senatours) that it feemeth abfurd and not likely to bee true, that they in their publike Affembly would decree any thing againft the maieftie of fuch a Queene, whofe like Chriftendom hath not had in this age, nor any other happier in noble a&ts, or in length of reign, or fuperioricie in princely vertues, and yet that the fame her Maiefty fhould be vniuftly accufed, and without being heard, blamed, is a thing not to be taken in good part: for this amóg priuate men, was alwayes accounted vnreafonable, much more beeing done againft a Queene of fo great Maieftie; which hath fo well deferued of the King and his Kingdome. For it is apparent, that certaine yeeres paft, the warre which the Turke had prepared againft the faid king and Kingdome by her Highneffe interceffion ceafed, and peace was granted to the king and his Realme, by the benefite whereof they to this day enioy quietneffe, and peace in that Kingdome: The

K          like

like good turne the Queene did in the yeere 1553. to the Kings Father *Iohn* king of *Sweden*, when as hee as well by his Embaſſadours the Lord *Enick* of *Wiſenbroughe* his Couſin, *Andrew Kithe* Counſellour and *Raſchias* his Secretarie, as alſo by letters ſent vnto her Maieſtie, earneſtly entreated her Highneſſe, to ſend an Embaſſage into *Muſcouie*, to make interceſſion for a peace betweene the ſaid king, and the *Muſcouite*, which ſhe without delay willingly performed, and by her perſuaſion drew the *Muſcouite* to make peace with the ſaid K. vpon indifferent, & reaſonable conditions: Which two excellent benefices done by her Maieſtie, the one to the Father, the other to the ſonne, and to their kingdomes are therfore rehearſed, becauſe that in remembrance thereof, a better and more courteous courſe of proceeding might iuſtly haue been expected from the king, and from the Senatours of his kingdome, then by your Oration (it appeareth) was by them determined: Inſomuch, that if at the beginning of your inſtructions, it had not been ſet downe, that your Commiſſion was decreed vpon in the Aſſembly of the Realme, it might haue been ſuſpected, that ſome pointes of your ſaid Commiſſion, not to be liked, were compoſed by ſome Spaniards, and ſlanderous Ieſuites, of which Ieſuites it is ſaid ther is a great number ſpread through manie partes of the Kingdome of *Polone*, whoſe malicious raylings, are often caſt out in publike places againſt her Maieſtie, and this Kingdome without condigne puniſhment, or any reprehenſion at all: and therefore it may be the more likely to be true, that they as ſworne men to the king of Spaine, together with the Spaniardes of late entertained by the King, and heard in the publike Aſſembly of the Realme, haue procured this Embaſſage with theſe kinde of Commiſſions in fauour of the King of Spaine.

The ſecond point of your Embaſſage conteyneth a requeſt for free Nauigation, or trade into Spaine, which we deeme to be ſuch, as the king of Spaine himſelfe hath lately in ſerious maner recommeded for himſelfe: for this prohibition was not ſet forth by the Queenes Maieſtie before ſhe was of neceſſitie

cessitie compelled thereunto: leaft the King of Spaine, open
enemie to this Realme, fhould bee furnifhed with Armes,
fhips, and Ammunition with fuch facilitie, and in fuch great
abundance, as he was from the Maritime parts of Germanie,
by meanes whereof he might maintaine long warre againft
this realme, fo that if he could not get thefe aides, and helpes,
it is manifeft that hee fhould bee forced to leaue off warre
and offer peace not only to this Realme, but alfo to others, a-
gainft who he moft vniuftly maketh war, wheras therefore it
is plaine, that this K. of Spaine, being an enemy to this realm,
is furnifhed, armed, and ftrengthened to continue this vniuft
war with fhips, victuall, and other warlike prouifions out of
certain cities vnder *Polone* & other maritime cities of Germany, in what fort can her Maiefty (being oppreffed by the Spaniard with vniuft war) tolerate or fuffer that fuch orders and
helpes fo openly & fo copioufly fhould be carried to the faid
K. her enemie for the continuance of warre againft her? And
although you many times repeate it, that the faid her Highnes
prohibitions were contrary to the law of nations, it is ftrange,
that you would al'eagde this againft the law of Nature, when
as by nature it felfe, it is ordeined, that euery man may defend
himfelfe againft force, which law not written, but borne with
vs wee haue not learned but receiued, and drawen from Nature it felfe, befides it is prouided by the ancient lawes to forbid, yea to let, and hinder, that no man minifter Armes,
victuall, or any thing elfe, whereby the enemie may bee holpen to make warre, as by this one, wherewith many other a-
gree, you may perceiue: *Cotem ferro fubigendo neceffariam,* H.lib.39.tit 4.
de Publicanis.
*Hoftibus quoque venundari vt ferrum & frumentum & Sales*
*non fine periculo capitis licet*: Neither may it here bee omitted,
that this prohibition is plainely contained in diuers Articles
of the Charters, giuen to the *Hanfes* by the Kings of Englande, and firft in the Charter of King *Edward* the firft
King of Englande, in thefe wordes following: *Licebit prae-*
*dictis Mercatoribus quo voluerint tam infra regnum & pote-*
*ftatem noftram, quàm extra Mercantias fuas ducere, feu portari*
*facere, praeterquam ad terras manifeftorū, & notoriorum Hoftiū*

*Regni nostri:* the very same clause, and promise is in expresse
words conteyned in the Charters of *Edward* the second, and
*Hernie* the sixth, kings of England, which exceptions so often times repeated by so many Kings, ought to admit no
reason to the contrarie, especially on those mens behalfe
who challenge their right by vertue of the said Charters onely: but we should haue had no neede to propounde these our
reasons vnto you, but that wee supposed you were ignorant
how this question of prohibiting ayd to be giuen to the king
of Spaine for making warre against vs, was handled about
two yeeres agoe before your King in his Counsaile, when as
certaine Merchants or Marriners of *Danzicke,* complained of
the like prohibition, and had obtained an Edict against her
Maiesties people, which Edict beeing oppugned with many
reasons by our Ambassadour Doctor *Parkins* heere present,
was abrogated and made void, so that there followed no execution vpon the same, but the *Danzickers* were dismissed:
which happened in the yeere 1595. so that to treat further of
this matter, wee should seeme to doe that, which is alreadie
done: yet we doe not denie, that which is alledged by some
on your behalfe, that these prohibitions are hurtfull to your
people, for that while the same are in force, they cannot with
their profite sell their Corne, and many other things growing in their Country: but for this is an easier remedie, if your
people wold bring a great part of the goods by her Maiesty
prohibited into this Realme of England. where it should bee
lawfull for them to sell the same with all fauour, and with their
great gaine, and carry another part thereof into the Lowe
Countreys and France, or into Italie, so it bee done without
fraud, and that the same come not into the Spaniardes Countrey: and by this meanes they may carry out and transport
all their goods safe, to the greater benefite of all the subiects
of *Polone* then otherwise, which might bee prooued mani-
festly by diuers examples, and presently by this, that
by carrying their Commodities into other Countreys
besides Spaine, they should auoide the arresting of their
Shippes, which happeneth euery yeere in that Countrey:

so

so that many times, to their great charge they are compelled to rigge their ships, and fit them for warlike vse, and so with eminent danger to hazard the losse of ships, and men in fight at sea, as too often the Danzickers and others haue proued: and euen this present sommer, it is knowne, that the Commanders of the Spanish Nauie haue hung vp and drowned in the Hauen of *Ferole* manie Mariners, Maisters and Pilotes of ships pertaining to the Maritime Cities of the *Hanses*, for that they went about to deliuer themselues, and their ships from violent and constrained bondage. For the auoiding of the like losse and dammage, her Maiestie this last yeare by publike writing set forth in the Dutch, French, & Latin tongue, declared, & gaue warning, that if there were any ships of forreigne Nations by any meanes, either with, or against their will, detained in the Spanish armie by sea, at that time ready to inuade England, it should be lawful for them, for their safety, to withdraw themselues out of the said Armie to ours, or to depart home quietly to their own Ports, without any dammage to be done vnto them by her Maiesties people: & it is certain that many ships, as well of *Danzicke*, as of *Hamburgh*, were found detained by the Spaniards amongst their ships, which the Englishmen of warre did their best to saue from burning when they did set fire on the Spanish Nauie: and if the King of Polones Counsellers had knowne of this writing, it had not bene congruent, that without mention of such a benefit done to the kings subiects, they should prosecute these matters in the worser part: neither can we here passe ouer in silence, that before her Maiesty did put the foresaid prohibitions in execution, she manie wayes made it knowne, as well by publike letters, as also by Admonition of the East country Merchants, that she now was of necessitie compelled for the defence of her Realme against the King of Spaine her open enemie, to forbid the transporting of Armes, Victuall, and other things into Spaine, wherewith the said King might set forth and furnish his Nauies, and Armies, and without the which he could not possibly continue the warre against this Realme. Besides all this for the iustifying and defence of the said her Maiesties

prohi-

prohibitions, it manifeftly appeareth, that the verie like haue beene often made by other Kings, and namely by the King of Polones father *Iohn* king of *Sweden*, and by *Sigifmond* King of Polone, grandfather to the King that now is, who by force took much merchandife from her Maiefties fubiects, for that they were to be caried into Mufcouie, which manie honeft Englifh Merchants, hereby brought into pouerty, haue caufe to remeber. The like was alfo oftentimes done by the Kings of Sweden to the fubiects of Denmark, who would haue traded into Mufcouie. And for confirmation hereof we can fhew the authentike Commiffions of the faid king *Sigifmond*, giuen to his Admirall *Otto Mannickes*, the 25. of May. 1566. and others of the 12. of March 1569. to *Afmo Genricke*, & the like to *Hans Necker*, Captaines of his, to whom authority was giuen vnder the faid Kings hand and feale, to intercept, take, fpoyle, and make hauocke of all thofe, which by way of merchandife, or otherwife, fhould carie into Mufcouie Powder, Ordinance, Saltpeter, Victuall, or any other kind of ware tending to warlike prouifion. There be alfo letters extant, written in verie earneft maner by the faid King *Sigifmond* vnto her Maieftie, dated in March, 1568. wherein by many arguments he fhewed, that the Traffike, or Nauigation into Sweden, and the *Narne*, forbidden to all men in generall, was moft iuft and lawfull, and by that meanes had prouided, that his enemies the Mufcouites fhould not be furnifhed, and armed not only with armes, weapons, & ammunition, but with other greater matters, which might helpe his enemie, and to that end he writeth, that he had fet a watch in the fea of men of war, with commandement, that if any man againft their will would trade into Mufcouie, they fhould take, and feaze vpon him, and all his goods. Of this Prohibition the Counfellers of Polone cannot be ignorant, neither was that wife and prouident King herein to be reprehended. And after that thefe reafons were deliuered vnto the faid Embaffadour, hee was asked whether any thing could bee iuftly oppofed againft them, whereunto he anfwered, that he had none authoritie to difpute of thefe matters, but onely to lay forth, that which

he

he had in commiffion, and to require and anfwere thereunto: the faid Counfellers therefore thought it not fit to vfe any
longer fpeech on that behalfe. But to conclude, auouched
for a full anfwere of all that hath beene by the faid Embaffadour propounded, that feeing it is manifeft, that this deede of
her Maieftie is allowable; not onely by the law of Nature to
defend her felfe, but alfo by the expreffe ciuile law, & examples of the king of Sweden and Polone, efpecially by diuerfe
Charters of the Kings of England, therefore her faid Maiefty
could not be rightly accufed either of inuftice, or Iuftice denied in any her doings, for as (faid they) fhe hath alwayes pro-
feffed (taking the omnipotét God the fearcher of harts to her
witneffe) it was neuer in her mind to comit any thing againft
the faered rule of Iuftice, fo fhe will be readie to giue eare to
any complainant, either her owne fubiect, or ftraunger, and
by her Officers to do iuftice to the faid plaintife, according to
equitie and reafon: the which fhe will alfo performe towards
you, if you fhall recommend any expreffe caufe of any fubiect of the kingdome of Polone. For her Maieftie is fo readie,
to giue anfwer to *Pifman* of *Danzick*, who (as it is faid) followed you from thence, for the profecuting of certaine his futes
for iuftice, that if you did not in fuch hafte vrge your departure, we her Maiefties Counfellours, before your departure,
fhould haue authoritie, to heare and determine his faid futes,
according to reafon and equitie. And to make an end of this
long yet neceffary anfwer of ours to your obiections, for that
manie of the things publifhed in your Embaffage, may by
imputation be taken in ill part againft the honour and dignitie of her Maieftie, all which by our faid anfwere are plainly
proued to haue proceeded from your king ill informed, her
Maieftie with good reafon doth expect, that when her an-
fwers fhall before the King and the Senate of his Realme
bee compared with the complaints of the Complainers, the
faid Senate will prouide, that the truth of her Maiefties
Actions bee no leffe publike by fome meanes repaired, and
reftored, then the contrarie hath beene attempted by falfe
accufations, and the Kings publike Embaffage, that fo it may
ap-

appeare,that the king hath that regard of the preseruation of mutuall friendship,as her Maieſtie doth expect from a prince that is her confederate,and brother:this anſwer was made by their Honours abouesaid on the thirteenth of Auguſt 1597. at *Greenwich,* with the which the said Poliſh Embaſſadour departed,and heerin the queſtion betweene the Engliſh and the *Hanſes* is fully laid open, and anſwered, and their malice againſt the ſtate of the land plainly diſcouered:ſo that it were more then time,that they were reſtored,and ſatisfied in their vnreaſonable pretences, as ſome without due conſideration vnaduiſedly deſire. About this time,to wit,the firſt of Auguſt 1597. the Emperor continually called vpon by *Don Guillelmo S. Clement* ordinarie Ledger for the King of Spaine at *Prage,*& ſtirred vp as wel by the abouesaid Embaſſages,as by the importunate, and clamorous ſollicitations of the *Hanſes,* permitted a Mandate or Edict to be publiſhed and ſet vp in the Empire, the tenour whereof enſueth, taken out of a tranſlation of the said Mandat into the Netherlandiſh tonge,and printed *cum priuilegio* at *Bruſſelles,* to the greater and more enormous iniurie and reproach of her Maieſtie,& her Highneſſe actions, and of the Companie of Merchants Aduenturers,as no doubt their meaning was, that were the Authours and doers therof,and conſequently to make the whole Engliſh nation and name the more odious and condemned of all men,thereby alſo openly iuſtifying and making lawfull all the vniuſt,and vnlawfull attempts,and practiſes of the king of Spaine and his miniſters againſt her said Maieſtie, Realme, and people.

*The Emperours Mandat againſt the Merchants Aduenturers.* We *Rudolph* the ſecond, by the grace of God Elect Romane Emperour,&c. to all and ſingular Princes, Electours, Princes Spirituall and temporal,Prelates, Earles, Barons, &c. ſend friendſhip,fauour, and all good: Heretofore in the time of our right welbeloued grandfather & father,the Emperers *Ferdinand* and *Maximilian*( of famous memorie)as alſo in the time of our Reigne ouer the Empire, the confederate Dutch *Hanſe* Townes, and ſome others thereby intereſſed manie yeares together , and at ſundrie times and tides not onely at

our Court, but alſo at former meetings of the Empire, eſpe- *Falſis narratis*
cially at *Ansburgh* in the yeare 1582. and at *Regensbourgh* in *tacita & ſup-*
the yeare 1594. laſt paſt, haue in complaining wiſe declared *preſſa veritate.*
and ſhewed: That 300. yeeres ago, and aboue had obtained
and gotten notable priuiledges, immunities, freedomes, and
exemptions within the Realme of England, partly by the
eſpeciall grace and fauor of the kings of that Land, and partly with great ſummes of money, for the good and commoditie of the holy Empire, and the members of the ſame, and for
the aduancement of the generall Trade and Commerce,
which priuiledges, &c. they haue held and enioyed till now,
not without their great and notable charge, as hauing beene
graunted, approued & confirmed by fourteene Kings of England ſucceſſiuely, and in the yeare 1470 by foreknowledge
and conſent of theſtates of the Land both ſpiritual & tempo-
rall, made of the force, & nature of a perpetuall and irreuoca-
ble contract: whereupon they held their reſidence and Officers within the Citie of *London* in an houſe, or counter, called
the Dutch Guild hall, where they vſed to buy Cloth of the
ſubiects of the Crowne of England, and caried the ſame from
thence into Dutchland, by means wherof Engliſh Cloth was
to be bought good cheape throughout all the ſaid countrie of *Notwithſtanding*
Dutchland: from whence alſo on the other ſide, a Trade was *this good cheape*
driuen with all kind of wares ſeruing England, to the no ſmal *the Lantgraues*
profite and gaine, as well of vs, as of the ſubiects of the Em- *of Heſſen had at*
pire, and of the Crowne of England. Which notwithſtanding *England 600.*
certaine couetous Companies of Merchants, whereof ſome *Clothes for their*
call themſelues Merchants Aduenturers, ſeeking their owne *Liueries which*
priuat gaine and lucre, are ſprung vp in the ſaid Realme, who *they would not*
by bad meanes haue wrought and practiſed, to the great and *haue bought*
notorious hurt and damage of the forſaid *Hanſes*, and haue *ſes had ſold Cloth*
taken vpon them to bring in many vntolerable innouations *ſo good cheape, as*
contrarie to the aboueſaid old Cuſtomes Priuiledges, and *heere is ſaid.*
perpetuall contract, obtained, and purchaſed with the great
coſts and charges of the ſayd *Hanſes*: So that it is come to
paſſe, that the Queene of England now reigning, will not
any longer endure to confirme the ſaid *Hanſes* Priuiledges,

L                              and

and perpetuall contract, and now finally the last yeare to the further & more intollerable grieuance of the foresaid *Hanse* Townes (specially for that they found it not reasonable nor fit to yeeld vnto the said Merchants Aduenturers a residence according to their desire at *Hamburgh*) hath wholly forbidden, and cut off all priuiledged trade, both within and without the said Realme of England, therby the better to strengthen the trade of the aforesaid Aduenturers Companie, and to bring their Monopolish traffique into a full course and traine with English Cloth, and Commoditie in such forme and manner, as the Staplers Companie haue drawne the trade of English Wooll into their owne hands onely, which now is apparant, in that the *Hanses* cannot enioy their Priuiledges, & well purchased traffike, whereas on the other side, the English Aduenturers Companie encreaseth in number, to wit, in Dutchland, first at *Embden*, where they were receiued by the Earle of Eastfriseland that then was, and afterwards in other places more, and now presently at *Stade* within the Archbishopricke of *Bremen*, where they haue setled the Cloth trade, and haue drawne vnto themselues onely other Commerces and Commodities, which the Dutch Merchants in former times vsed to enioy: and further, to the preiudice of the *Hanse* Townes, haue erected an especiall societie, Staple, Colledge, Confederacie, and Alliance, by means whereof they haue not onely made diuerse and sundrie Monopolish Prohibitions, Treaties and Accordes, hurtfull to the common wealth of the holy Empire, against vs, and against the Right and ordinance of the said Empire, and against all vse of Merchants, but also haue raised Cloth, and other wares according to their owne willes, to such a dearenesse, *that the price thereof is almost as high againe, as it was wont to be when the *Hanses* might vse their Priuiledges. Besides, the said English Aduenturers do not sell their Clothes after they haue beene wet, and put in the water without retching, or stretching, as it ought to be by the policie, constitutions, and penall Statutes of the Holy Empire: and for that the same Hanses might ship cloth out of England as good cheape, as the M. M. Aduenturers

* How came it to passe the that diuerse Factors, & Seruants of sundrie the Princes Electors & Lords of the Empire, bought their liuerie clothes of the Merchants Aduenturers, at such time as the

hath

hath beene left ⸱ vnpunished a long time, other Merchants, which buy Cloth of the said Aduenturers, do take occasion of the like bad example. Finally, through the drift and dealing of these Aduenturers, the Dutch Merchant hath the best of his Trade taken from him: omitting heere how that the Queene of England with armed hand hath presumed, or aduanced her selfe, to cause the Merchants Aduenturers ships to be conuoyed from *London* to *Stade*, through the Dutch sea, and within ours, and the Holy Empires iurisdiction and commaundement: and besides, hath set vp and published all kind of Edicts tending to the hindrance, and impeaching of the freedome of the sea, and Nauigation, together with arrests which haue followed vpon the same, by meanes whereof the *Hanse* Townes, and other our subiectes, and the subiects of the Holy Empire, are forced to forsake, and leaue vnfrequented the foresaid free Nauigation throughout the whole ⸱ Westerne sea, and in the Ems streame, and partly in the Easterne sea, and else where: for which cause the foresaid *Hanse* Townes, and others thereby interessed, haue called vpon vs and the holy Empire, and in most humble manner haue prayed and besought vs to haue consideration of all these matters, and to giue them herein aid and assistance.

Forasmuch then, as we found, that these complaintes and grieuances were of verie great weight and importance, and seeing that by our neighbourly, and friendly wrting to the Queene of England we haue but smally preuailed: and lastly, for that we haue litle profited with our Emperiall Mandate & ordinances heretofore set forth against the retainers of the said M.M. Aduenturers, but to the contrarie, perceiuing that for the defence and iustifying of these matters, all kind of disputations, excuses, questions, and delayes were moued and brought forth, it seemed to vs verie necessarie, before al other things, for our more assurance of the truth on this behalfe, to cause a diliget & perfect informatio to be taken, whether the English Aduenturers cōpany did vse any trade or Monopolies contrarie to our, and the holy Empires ordinances, which be-

*There are none who desire a reformation in this point more thē the M. M. Aduenturers*

*Vnto this the Hamburgers gaue occasion by exacting a tolle by forcible hand, laying their men of warre before the Swinge for that purpose: Defensio autem non tantùm omni iure est permissa, sed etiam pro defensione rerum & bonorum aliī non modo vulnerare, sed & occidere licet, & is qui illicitè exactam gabellam soluere recusat, neque Deū, neq; homines offendit*

*Vnto this see her Maiesties answer made to the Polish Embassador.*

*It were reason the M.M. Aduenturers were heard what they could obiect to this deposition.*

ing done,it was found by the depofition of not a few credible
perfons at *Francfort* vpon *Main*,in the Lent Mart 1581. and
by other information on this behalfe taken, that all that is a-
boue written clearely appeared:and that which is more, that
the aforefaid Aduenturers Colledges were heretofore forbidden,and banifhed out of *Danzicke* in Pruffia,as alfo out of

* How the M.M.
Aduenturers
were banifhed
out of the Burgü-
difh low Coütries,
appeareth before,
and if they be not
now banifhed
out of the Em-
pire by the pra-
ctife of the fame
men the Spanifh
Minifters, let the
wife iudge.

fome places of the low * Burgundifh, and other Countries :
Wnereupon hauing with our felues weighed the whole matter,according to the importance thereof,and confidered,that
thefe things concerned not onely the *Hanfe* Townes,but alfo
all the fubiects and Merchants of the holy Empire,the further
proceeding therin was deferred to a generall affembly of the
Empire,holden at *Ausburgh* in the yeare 1582.againft which
we caufed the Acts and propofitions concerning the fame,
to be fent vnto all the Princes Electors, to the end, that they
might the ripelier and better confider vpon the fame,and afterwards we laid the matter in deliberation of all the States of
the holy Empire: who after mature counfell,and bethinking,
gaue vs their aduife and opinions vpon the fame, praying vs
withall , that feeing there was no meanes to obtaine at the
forefaid Queene of Englands hands the full reftitution of the
forefaide *Hanfes* priuiledges, hereditarie agreement, & contract, and that in the meane while the Englifh Aduenturers
Companie vfed, and went forward with an hurtfull Monopoly,againft all right and reafon,that we would with publike
Edicts,forbid the forefaid Merchants Aduenturers their trade
by water, and by land, throughout the holy Empire, and the
iurifdiction and command of the fame. And further,that we
would ftraightly charge,and vpon great penalties enioyne e-
uerie State,whom it might concerne, not to permit the faid
M. M. Aduenturers, or their Conforts, confederated Companies,factors and feruants,to haue recourfe or any common
Traffike in any place within the holy Empire, but rather to
expell,defend,and forbid the fame, vpon paine of our indig-
nation,and loffe of all Royalties,Fiefes,Rights and iurifdicti-
ons, which to the difobedient on this behalfe might apper-
taine or belong, either vnder vs or the Holy Empire.

And

And if fo be, that contrary to this our Emperial commandement, the English Merchants Aduenturers, or their factors
or feruants, fhold be fo bold, as to yfe or driue any trade either
in buying or felling of English clothes, Wooll or other wares
what foeuer, at any place within the holy Empire, that then
each Magiftrate & Ruler within his command or iurifdiction,
fhold be holden where the faid bought or fold goods may be
found, & where fuch trade is vfed, prefently to feaze vpō and
confifcate the faid forbidden goods, as by the contents of the
aduife, and determination to vs at that time deliuered at *Auf-
burghe* on the behalf of the Electors, princes and States ofthe
holy Empire more at large appeareth; howbeit wee proceeded not to the publifhing of the faid Mandates, but notwith-
ftanding that the Deputies of the faid *Hanfe* townes earneftly infifted to haue a finall conclufion of this matter, we firft of
all fought by al gentle meanes, to induce, & moue the Queen
of England, for the confirmation of good neighbourhood, to
giue vs and the Empire, as alfo the *Hanfe* townes contentment in the aboue-written complaints & grieuances, without
compelling vs for that caufe to vfe any fharper meanes, or remedie; and to that end we gaue her Ambaffador, at that time
being at *Afburghe*, to vnderftand, through what vrgent and
neceffarie occafions the forefaid Mandate was concluded, &
refolued vpon by vs and the States of this holy Empire, and
withall to offer that whenfoeuer it fhould like the Queene
of England, to fuffer the matter to bee brought to a friendly
treatie and communication, and to that ende fhould appoint
her Embaffadours with full Commiffion, that we then on the
otherfide would be willing to depute alfo certaine perfonages
of qualitie, & countenance, before whom both parties fhould
appeare at fome conuenient place within the Empire, and lay
forth their doleances, and griefes, and fo grow to a compofi-
tion and determination in all reafon, & with a true and faithfull heart and meaning : We alfo admonifhed, & finally moued the *Hanfe* townes to their great coft and charges to fend
a perticular Legation into England vnto the Queene, where
after they had prefented our letters of Interceffion, which we

L 3                                     gaue

gaue them with them, a friendly agreement, and compositi-
on was required, but they could not effect or profit any thing
on this behalfe, but receiued of the Queene a cleane contrarie answere. In the meane while the Aduenturers with their
Monopolish trade and dealings encreased more and more,
and multiplied in the Empire, and ouer, and aboue this, the
English did vnto the subiectes of vs, and the holy Empire in
the open sea, great violence and damage : Which discom-
moditie began, continued, & encreased whole twelue yeres
long, to wit, from the Assembly at *Ausbourghe*, 82. to the Assembly last held at *Regensbroughe* 94. to the preiudice and
contempt not onely of our Emperiall Intercession, but also
of the writing of the *Hanse* townes, and of the many wayes
sought for the friendly appointment, in so much that the
*Hanse* townes, at the last holden Assembly at *Rigensbroughe*,
againe complained on this behalfe, and wee considering the
manifest necessitie of the cause, laid the same a fresh in deliberation, and consultation with the Electours, Princes, and
States which then appeared, and with the Counsellours, Am-
bassadours, and Deputies of the Princes which appeared not
personally at the said Assembly : And for as much, as it was
found to be against all right and reason, that the *Hanses* shold
be spoiled in the Realme of England of all their Iust title,
hereditarie agreement and Priuiledges gotten, as aforesaide
with their great cost and charges, and that on the other side
the M.M. Aduenturers with their Conuenticles, Compa-nie

*Contractus sunt*
*de Iure Gentium*
*liberi: & vt li-*
*beri sunt, ita eti-*
*am ignorante*
*Magistratu ex*
*generali legum*
*conessione cum*
*quouis non hoste*
*libere & licite*
*exerceantur.*

and traine, without any * permission of vs as presently raign-
ing Romaine Emperour and supreme head of the holy Empire, yea, that which is more, contrarie to all former recesses,
and Mandates, should *de facto* intrude themselues and goe
through with their trade, to the notable losse and damage of
all the States of this Empire great and small, and to the bringing in of a dearth in Cloth and Wooll, & by their Monopolish practises (which according to the constitutions of vs and
the holy Empire deserue great punishment) to goe about to
weaken, and ouerthrow the ancient and honest trade of Merchandise vsed among the laudable Dutch Nation : without
making

making mention in this place of the outrage, force and violence, which the aforesaid English had committed, with manifold robberies, & spoilings at sea, to the dangerous conse-
quence and preiudice of the iurisdiction, & superiority which
pertaineth and belongeth to vs and the holy Empire in the
same: therefore in the foresaid assembly of the Empire, it was
with one voyce and consent concluded and resolued of vs by
the Electors, princes & States required, that if so be (notwithstanding all the great paines & charges hitherto in vaine bestowed) at our new instance & requisition with deduction of
all the circumstances thereto necessary, the Queene of England would not let the *Hanse* townes inioy their Priuiledges
free, certaine, and whole, as heretofore of old they had them,
and would not also suffer the Commerce, & trade open, and
vnmolested, that then wee should indeed assist the *Hanse*
townes, as the faithfull subiectes of vs, and the holy Empire,
and should cause the aboue-mentioned Mandate agreed
vpon at *Ausboroughe* 1582. to be published and put in execution against the hurtfull Monopolish Company of the M.M.
Aduenturers, without any sauour, dissimulation, or composi-
tion: which Consultation in such maner by the Electours,
Princes, & States in generall, with one consent propounded,
at former Assemblies, & now againe renued, were according
to right and reason confirmed and ratified, and consequently the fifth of Iuly 1595. wrote vnto the aforesaid Queene
louingly, and neighbourly requiring her a newe, and setting
before her eies the aforsaid reasons, with many other motiues
thereto seruing, that she would cause the old, and continuall
complaints, together with the oppressions & damages of the
*Hanse* townes to cease, but we receiued such an answere vnto
this our writing, that therby jt may sufficiently be perceiued,
that our hetherto long vsed patiēce is not only receiued with
small thanks, but withal the sayd Q presumeth, to ascribe vnto her self some interest herein, & to draw the same into con-
sequence, as though by our deferring of the publishing of the
said Mandates, the intrusion of the aforesaid M.M. Aduenturers were allowed, or that it stood in the liking, choyce, will,

                                                        and

and power of the Queene, to take from the aforefaid *Hanfe* townes their dearly purchafed liberties, & hereditary accord, and fo wil not that in any other place then in England (where fhee may bee iudge and partie) that any treatie bee held on this behalfe, and befides requiring that her fubiects according to their owne good liking and pleafure may haunt, liue, and exercife their Marchandife within the Empire of the Dutch nation, which for vs and the Empire it falleth altogether grieuous, and very contumelious to diffemble any longer: therefore then, whereas wee in regard of our Emperiall office and place, cannot any longer delay to put in execution the aforefaid confultations, and Decrees of the yeeres 82. and 94. for the furtherance of the common welfare, and for neceffities fake, efpecially feeing the Monopolies, & preiudiciall, dangerous & vnlawfull foreftalling (which as is aboue faid, are vied among the Englifh Aduenturers Companie) by teftimonies and other credible informations, are altogether open and manifeft, and not only according to the common written lawes, but alfo according to the publifhed Conftitutions of the Empire, are forbidden vpon great penaltie and punifhment, to wit, loffe of goods and chattell, and banifhment out of the land.

Therefore is it that we prohibite, banifh out, and profcribe all the forenamed Englifh M.M to wit, the whole companie of the M.M Aduenturers, together with their hurtful dealings, trafficks, and contractings out of all the holy Empire, fo that fuch hurtfull Commerces, and dealings of the Englifh Aduenturers, with the conuentions, compactes, and alliances on this behalfe made, from this time forwad fhall bee forbidden and made void, without that any man by himfelfe, or any other fhall or may hereafter exercife, or practife the fame or dayning therefore, & commanding exprefly by our Romifh Emperiall power and authoritie, according to the refolution of the Electors, Princes, and States of the Empire agreed vpon, renued, & approued, that vpon paine of the ban, and profcription of vs and the holy Empire, all & euery Merchants, and dealers in Englifh cloth (to the Companies of M.M. Aduenturers

uenturers any waies allyed or affociated)together with their
Factours, Agentes, Atturnyes, and feruants, that within three
months after the publifhing, & fetting forth of thefe prefents,
they depart and remoue without further delay, or oppofition
out of the rule, command, and land of vs, and of the holy Empire, as alfo of the Electours, and common States, and fpecial-
ly out of the towne of *Stade*, fituate in the Archbifhoprcke
of *Breme*, and out of all other partes and places, where they
commonly haue their refidence, and conuenticles, or exercife their Trade: and that from henceforward they wholly,
and entirely abftaine, and forbeare from all recourfe, & Commerces howfoeuer they may bee called by water & by land,
openly or priuily throughout all the whole Empire. And further we giue commandement to all Princes Electours, Princes, States and fubiects of vs and the holy Empire, vpon the
forfeiture of all their Royalties, Fiefs, and other rights, and
dueties obtained of vs, and the holy Empire (which euery
one whofoeuer fhall dare wilfully to doe here againft *ipfo fa-*
*cto* fhall forfeit) that they vnto the faid Englifh, naming
themfelues Merchants Aduenturers, their Societies, Companies, Factours and Seruantes, no where in the holy Empire
by land or by water, doe giue, yeeld, or permit any open, or
fecret conueighance paffage, helpe, or other fauour, but the
fame doe altogether let and prohibite: And if fo be that the
Englifh Aduenturers, their Adherentes, Factours, or Seruants boldly fhall go forward, or proceed, contrary to this our
Emperiall Mandate, and commaundement, either in buying or felling of Clothes and Wooll, or with exercifing any
other Commerces, howfoeuer they may bee called in any
quarter or place of the holy Empire, in fuch cafe, hereby authoritie and power is giuen, and earneftly is inioyned, and
required that all Magiftrates, and Rulers, vnder whofe command, or Iurifdiction fuch place immediatly doeth lye, and
where fuch kind of trade is vfed, or where fuch bought or fold
goods may be found, to apprehend the perfons without delay. and to arreft and confifcate the forbidden goods. And
further it fhall not be lawfull for any Magiftrate, or Ruler in

M                                        the

the Empire, to giue Conuoy, or safeconduct with whatsoeuer
words, meaning, colour, or clauses the said Conuoyes or safe-
condiuctes may be côceiued, or set down, to the English Aduenturers Companyes, Merchants or dealers, neither shall
they be conducted or conuoyed by any Magistrate, or Superiour in the said Empire : and in case that the Magistrate, or
Superiour shall be herein negligent, or slacke, and that we, or
our Procurour Fiscaell shall be thereof aduertised, then our
will is, that the said Fiscael (according to our Commaundement to him in earnest maner already giuen) on this behalfe,
to advertise the Magistrate, or Superiour, where the said Merchauntes, and Dealers dwell, or reside, and admonishe the
same such Englishe trade foorthwith out of hande to forbid:
and if so bee the saide Magistrate, or Superiour, doe not so
within the prefixed tyme, we will on our Emperiall Courtes
parte, or otherwise our foresaid Fischale shall haue full power,
right, and authoritie to proceede to the execution of this our
Emperiall Mandate, and by vertue of this his office presently
to call in question the disobédient, without all fauour or dissimulation, as the necessitie of the cause shal require, without
that it shall be lawfull for the aforesaid misdoers to alleadge,
or produce any exceptions, or declinatorie delay in any maner whatsoeuer. And for that it is lawful & permitted to euery
man to giue information agąinst the transgressours, therefore
whosoeuer first shall informe the Magistrate, where offence
is made of the said offence plainely and truely, or in case of
negligence in the said Magistrate, or Fiscaell, he shal haue the
fourth part of the offendours goods, wherein also he shall be
assisted, and holpen by the foresaid Magistrate, or Superiour,
or in default thereof by vs, and our Emperiall Chamber right,
and by all other States of the holy Empire : according to this
let euery man take knowledge, howe to demeane himselfe.
Giuen in our Royall Castell at *Praghe,* the first day of the
moneth of August. *Anno* 1597. of our Romish Kingdome
the 22. yeere, of *Hungarie* the 25. and of *Bohemia* also the 22.
Subscribed *Rudolph,* Paragraphed *I.D.W. Freymondt, ad Mandatum Sacræ Cæsareæ Maiestatis proprium,* And signed *An
Han-*

*Hanniwalt:* and the priuie feale of the Emperors Maieſtie was printed vpon the ſame in forme of a *Placcart* or *Ediϛ.*

Theſe are the words of the Mandate, which I haue fully & truely ſet downe, to the end that it may the better appeare, what the cauſes were of the ſaid Mandat, & what good frieds the *Hanſes* are to the ſtate of England. Cöcerning the cauſes, I note them to be three in number: Firſt, *The taking away of the Eaſterlinges Priuiledges in England.* Secondlie, *The doings of the Englishmen of warre at the Sea.* And thirdlie, *The Monopolie vſed by the Merchantes Adventurers.* To the firſt two cauſes her Maieſtie at ſundrie times hath ſufficientlie anſwered, and namely by her Letters written to the Emperour in the yeares 1585. and laſtlie, by the anſwere giuen to the Poliſh Embaſſadour, as aboue at large is ſet downe. As for the Monopoly, wherewith the Merchants Adventurers are charged, it is but a meere ſlaunder, and iniurious imputation, maliciouſlie deuiſed by the *Hanſes,* to bleare the eies of the States, & Princes of the Empire withall, and to drawe them vnder colour of complayning on the M.M. Adventurers, as Monopoliſhe traders, to ayde, and affiſte the ſaide *Hanſes,* to recouer their Pruiledges againe, and to maintaine them therein, conttarie to all reaſon againſt the Engliſh Nation, as I doubt not anone moſt plainly, & clearely to proue.

Her Maieſtie being enformed of the aboueſaid Mandate, ſent Maiſter *Iohn Wrothe,* & Maiſter *Stephen Leſieur,* with letters to the Emperour, and diuerſe of the Electours, and Princes of Germanie, declaring her Highnes opinion of this proceeding as an vniuſt practiſe and doing of the *Hanſes,* and therefore required to haue the ſaid Mandate reuoked, or ſuſpended, but being vncertain, what would follow hereupon, it ſeemed good vnto her Maieſtie in the mean time, to direct a commiſſion to the Maior, and Sheriffes of the Cittie of London, in maner following.

E *Lizabeth* by the grace of God Queen of Englãd, France, and Ireland, Defender of the faith, &c. To our right truſtie & welbeloued the Maior, and Sheriffes of our Citie of *London* greeting. Wheras there hath bin directed a Commandment by the name of a Mandate, from the Romaine Emperour to all Electors, Prelates, Earles and all other Officers, and subiectes of the Empire, reciting sundry complaintes made to him by the allied Townes of the Dutch *Hanses* in Germany, of diuers iniuries committed againſt them in our Realme, and likewiſe vpon complaint made by them againſt the companie of M.M. Aduenturers, without hearing any anſwere to bee made to the ſaide *Hanſe* Townes in diſproofe of their complaints, the ſame being moſt notorious, vniuſt, and not to be mainteyned by any trueth. And yet neuertheles by this Mandate the Engiliſh Marchants, namely the M. M. Adueturers are forbidden to vſe any trafficke of Merchandiſe within the Empire, but are commanded to depart from thence vpon paines, & to forbeare openly and ſecretly from all hauens, and landing places, or to vſe any Commerce by water or by land in the Empire, vpon paine of apprehenſion of their perſons, & confiſcation of their goods, with ſundry other extreme ſentēces pronounced againſt our ſaid ſubiects; hereupon, although we haue ſent our letters expreſly to the Emperor and to the Electors and other Princes of the Empire, declaring our opinion of this proceeding, to be vniuſtly proſecuted by the ſaid *Hanſe* Townes, and therefore haue required to haue the ſaide Mandate either reuoked or ſuſpended, yet being vncertaine what ſhall follow hereupon, we haue thought it agreeable to our honour in the meane time, to commaund all ſuch as are here within our realm, appertaining to the ſaid *Hanſe* towns, ſituate in the Empire, and eſpecially all ſuch as haue any reſidence in our citie of London, either in the houſe commonly called the Steelyard, or in any other place elſewhere, do forbeare to vſe any maner of trafficke of Merchandiſe, or to make any contractes, and likewiſe to depart out of our Dominions in like ſort, as our ſubiects are commanded to depart out of the Empire, vpon the like paines, as are conteyned againſt our ſubiectes in the ſaide Mandate. And for the execution of this our Commaundement, wee will, that you the Maior of our ſaid Citie of London, and the Sheriffes, ſhall foorthwith repaire to the houſe, called the Steelyarde,

and

and calling before you fuch, as haue charge thereof, or do refide there, to giue them knowledge of this our determination and commaundement : Charging them by the foure and twentieth day of this moneth (being the day that our Merchants are to depart from *Stade*) they do depart out of this Realme : charging them alfo, that they giue knowledge thereof to fuch as be of any of the *Hanfe* Townes belonging to the Empire, remaining to any part of our Realme, to depart likewife by the faid day. And you the Maior and Sheriffes, calling vnto you two of the officers of our Cuftomhoufe, to take poffeffion of the faid houfe the faid. 24. day, to remaine in our cuftodie, vntill we fhall vnderftand of any more fauourable courfe taken by the Emperour, for the reftitution of our fubiects to their former lawfull trade within the Empire, and this fhall be your warrant for the execution of the Premifes. In witneffe whereof wee haue caufed thefe our Letters to be made patent : Witneffe our felfe at *Weftminfter* : the thirteenth of Ianuarie in the fortieth yeere of our Reigne.

In this ftate the matters haue hung euer fince, the M. M. Aduenturers ftill expecting a Diete, or generall Affembly of the Princes and States of the Empire, in hope that by her Maiefties gracious interuention for them, the abouefaid Mandat may be either abrogated, or fufpended, and they reftored to their former trade, and priuiledges in the Empire, for without fuch an affembly this cannot be done, (as appeareth plainely by the anfwer of the Emperor, & Princes vnto thofe Letters which it pleafed her Highneffe to write by the abouefaide Maifter *Wroth* and Maifter *Lefieur*) and on the other fide the *Hanfes* ftil laboring to haue the abouefaid Mandate extended and ftretched further then the contents thereof will beare, to wit, that all Englifhmen generally, and all Englifh wares, fhould be banifhed and forbidden the Empire: for that otherwife they fee, that they loofe their labour and coft, and the Merchants Aduenturers find means to continue their trade, and to vent the Commodities of their Country in Germany, maugre all that their Aduerfaries & ill willers can do, though

M 3                              not

not in that fort that were conuenient, but becaufe you fhall see, what caufe the *Hanfes* haue to complaine in fuch clamorous maner, as they do of iniuries done them in this Realme, I will giue you the view of a Decree of the right Honourable priuy Counfell, giuen at *Weftminfter* the 24. day of Februarie in the fixt yeare of the reigne of King *Edward* the fixt, in thefe words following.

*Decree againft the Hanfes in the reigne of K. Edward the fixth.*

In the matter touching the Information exhibited againft the Merchantes of the *Hanfe*, commonlie called the Merchauntes of the Steelyard, vpon good confideration, as well of the faid Information, as alfo of the anfwere of the faid Merchants of the Steelyard, and of fuch records, Writings, Charters, Treaties, Depofitions of witneffes, and other recordes and proofes, as hath beene exhibited on both parties, it was found apparant to the Kings Maiefties priuie Councel as followeth.

Firft, it is found, that all liberties and priuiledges pretended to be graunted to the faid Merchants of the *Hanfe* bee void by the lawes of the Realme, forafmuch as the fame Merchants of the *Hanfe* haue no fufficient Corporation to receiue the fame. It appeareth alfo, that fuch graunt, and Priuiledges, as the faid Merchaunts of the *Hanfe* do claime to haue, doe not extende to anie perfons, or Townes certaine, and therfore vncertain what perfons, or which townes fhould enioy the faid priuiledges: by reafon of which vncertaintie, they haue, & do admit to be free with them whom & as many as they lift, to the great preiudice & hurt of the kings Maiefties Cuftomes, & yeerely hinderance of twentie thoufand poundes, or neere thereabouts, befides the common hurt to the whole realme. It appeareth alfo, that if the pretended grants were good by the lawes of the Realme, as indeed they be not, yet the fame were made vpon condition, that they fhould not auow, or colour any forreignes goods or merchandifes, which condition the Merchants of the *Hanfe* haue not obferued, as may appear by office found remaining of record in the Kings Maiefties Exchequer, and by other fufficient proofes of the fame. It appeareth alfo, that one hundred

dred

dred yeares, and more, after the pretended priuiledges granted to them, the foresaid Merchants of the *Hanse* vsed to transport no Merchandise out of this Realme, but onely into their owne countries, neither to bring into this Realme anie wares, or merchandise, but onely such as were commodities of their owne Countries: where at this present they do not only conueigh the Merchandise of this Realme into the base countries of *Brabant, Flaunders*, and other places neare adioining, and there sell the same, to the great dammage, and subuersion of the laudable order of the Kings Maiesties subiects, trading those parties for Merchandise, but also do bring into this Realme, the Merchandise, and comodities of all forreigne Countries, contrarie to the true meaning of the graunts of their Priuiledges, declared by the ancient vsage of the same: by meanes whereof the Kings Maiestie hath not onely lost much in his Customes, but also it is contrarie to the conditions of a Recognisance, made in the time of King *Henrie* the seuenth. It appeared also, that like as the Priuiledges heretofore graunted to the said Merchants of the Steelyard, being at the beginning reasonably vsed, were commodious and much profitable vnto them, without any notable, excessiue, or enorme preiudice to the royall estate of this Realme, so now of late yeares, by taking of such, and so manie as they list into their societie, and by bringing in the commodities of all other Countries, as carrying out the comodities of this realm into al other places, their said pretesed priuiledges are growne so preiudiciall to the King & his crowne, as without the great hurt thereof, and of the whole estate of this Realme, the same may not be long endured.

Item, in the time of King *Edward* the fourth, the said Merchants of the Hanse forfeited their pretended priuiledges by meanes of warre betweene this Realme and them, whereupon a Treatie was made, and agreed, that the subiects of this Realme should haue like liberties in the land of *Prusse*, and other places of the Hanse, as they had, and ought to haue vsed there, and that no imposts, newe exictions, or other prestes should be set vpon their persons, or goods otherwise, or by

other

other meane,then before ten,twentie,thirtie,fortie,fiftie,yea
an hundred yeares agoe, and aboue had beene, or were set,
which hath beene,and is daily much broken, and specially in
*Danzicke*,not only by prohibiting English men freely to buy
and sell there,but also in leuying vpon them certaine exactions, and impositions, contrarie to the said Treatie : And notwithstanding,that diuerse requests haue beene made, as well
by the Kings Maiesties Father,as by his Maiestie, for the present redresse of such wrongs as haue beene done to the English Merchants, contrarie to the said Treatie, yet no reformation hath hetherto ensued. In consideration of which the
premises,and such other matters as hath appeared in the examination of this matter,the Lords of the Kings Maiesties priuie Counsell, on his Highnesse behalfe decreed, That the
Priuiledges, Liberties and Franchises claimed by the foresaid
Merchants of the Steelyard, shall from henceforth be and remaine seazed, and resumed into the Kings Maiesties handes,
vntill the said Merchants of the Steeleyard shall declare, and
proue better and more sufficient matter for their claime in
the premises,sauing and reseruing vnto the said Merchants of
the Steeleyard all such, and like liberties of comming into this
Realme,and other the Kings Dominions, buying, selling,all
and all maner of traffike and trade of Merchandise in as large
and ample maner,as any other Merchants strangers haue, or
of right ought to haue within the same. This order aforesaid,
or anie thing herein contained to the contrarie notwithstan-
ding.This Decree was firmed by *T. Ely Chauncellour, Win-
chester, Northumberland, Bedford, Westmerland, Shrewsburie,
E. Clinton, T.Darcie, N.Wutton,* and *W. Cecill.* By the contents whereof, a man may plainely see, that whatsoeuer
happened to the *Hanses* in England, they themselues gaue
the occasion thereof,and therfore had no iust or lawfull cause
to complaine. Notwithstanding Queene *Marie* by the way
of Recesse,the land being full of troubles, reuoked this Decree, and restored the *Hanses* to their former priuiledges, in
the moneth of Aprill An.1553.at which time the *Hanses* had
their Commissioners in England about a Treatie offered by
King

King *Edward,* and accepted by the *Hanses* after the abouesaid resumption, whereunto she was reduced for two reasons:
the one was, for that the *Hanses* Commissioners promised,
that their inordinate trade, forbidden by the lawes of the
land, and their too too much frequenting the low Countries,
should be left: The other was, for that by meanes of the dan-
gerousnes & hardnes of the time, the abouesaid Decree of the
resumption of the *Hanses* Priuiledges, could not be dealt in:
but this promise of the Commissioners not being performed,
the said Queene in the yeare 1556. caused her foresaid Re-      *Renocation of the*
uocation to be altered, and by a Decree restrained the *Hanses*  *foresaid Renoca-*
                                                               *tion.*
trade in the low Countries with Cloth, and their bringing in
of any other forreigne wares, then those of their owne lands
only, suffering them notwithstanding in other points, to vse
their pretensed Priuiledges: and afterwards by mediation of
King *Philip,* yeelding to a further moderation, with condition
that the *Hanses* within one yeare next ensuing, should send
their Commissioners into England, to confer, treat, and conclude with her Highnesse Coūsellors, in what sort their Priuiledges ought to be taken and vsed. A whole yeare passed, and
fiue weeks besides without any newes or tidings of any commissioners, and to requite the manifold fauours they had receiued, they at an Assembly of the *Hanses* at *Lubeck,* published an Edict against all English men forbidding all trade or
Commerce with them, and staying the carrying out of
Corne, which was prouided for the seruice and necessitie
of the Realme: yet for all these indignities, the said Queene
was contented that Commissaries on both parts should meet
in England, and agree vpon, and set downe a certaine and
immutable manner of Trade to be held, and obserued on
both parts sides: but the *Hanses* were so farre from accep-
ting of this gracious offer, that they wholly refused it, as by
a petition of theirs exhibited to King *Philip,* the third of Iune
1557. appeareth, wherein they declare the cause of that
their refusall to bee, for that they coulde not haue in this
Realme anie other iudges of their cause, but such as were
suspected, not sparing, or excepting the Queene her selfe, of
                     N                              whose

whose good will and fauour, they had receiued so often experience and triall. In these tearmes the *Hanses* Priuiledges stoode all Queene *Maries* dayes, after whose deceafe her Maiestie that now is, succeeding, and finding them as they were left without any other ground or foundation, then the Princes fauour and good pleasure, yet at the sollicitation of *Suiderman*, and others, Commissioners from the *Hanses*, her Highnesse was contented, that a meeting and communication should be held in the yeare 1560. whereas the *Hanses* stood and insisted vpon their old Treaties: and those appointed by her Maiestie propounded certaine other Articles, intituled, *A moderation of the olde Priuiledges.* with this clause of singular fauour. *Neque tamen excellentissima Regina propter hanc Moderationem ab vllo superiori legitimo Iure vlla ex parte recedi vult, sed saluum ius, saluas actiones, saluam denique reliquam omnem in hac Commercii causa materiam, & sibi ex altera parte, & suis successoribus, & ex altera parte Confederatis Ciuitatibus, & eorum posteritati reseruat.* But the Hanses Commissioners not liking thereof, the Treatie brake vp without any effect. In which tearmes the matter hung till the yeare 1572. at which time new Commissioners from the *Hanse* Townes comming into England for other causes, they renewed their former suit and petition: whereunto they receiued this answere, That concerning the Custome of their goods, there should nothing more be exacted of them, then was propounded to the former Commissioners in the yeare 1560. All this while her Maiesties subiects were depriued of all priuiledge, and in diuerse of the Hanse Townes hardly and extreamly vsed, as at *Dansicke, Deuenter, Campen* and *Swoll*, to the great hurt and hinderance of the trade: and because the Hanses vnmeasurably frequented the City of *Antwerpe* with English Commoditie, the Merchants Aduenturers were forced to draw themselues wholy to the said Citie, and leaue *Berghen ap Zoom*, where they vsed to keepe two Marts in the yeere: But finally the said Aduenturers were forced to leaue *Antwerpe* also, and to seeke another place, as hath beene aboue rehearsed: so that in the yeare

1567.

*Mater passed betweene her Maiestie and the Hanses.*

**1567.** they obtained Pnuiledges for ten yeares of the Town of *Hamburgh* with this condition thereunto added. *Quod ela-psis supradictis annis concessio dictorum Priuilegiorum renouare-tur, & continuaretur in infinitum, si interim non cederet in Ciui-tatis sue damnum, vel dispendium.* That the ten yeres time be-ing expired, the foresaid Pnuiledges should be renewed, and continued for euer, if in the mean while no hurt, or dammage happened to their Citie thereby. But for all this, when the ten yeares were almost complete and run out, the Hamburgers signified to the Merchants Aduéturers, that the time of their Priuiledges expired, & that by a Decree of the Hanse townes made at *Lubeke*, they were enioyned, not to grant to the said Aduenturers anie longer Priuiledges, pretending the cause to be, for that in England the said Hanses were restrained of their ancient liberties, and that daily new exactions were imposed vpon their goods, cótrarie to former Treaties: which done, the said Hamburgers passed a Decree the 20. of Iune, **1578.** whereby they abrogated all former liberties granted to the said Aduenturers, and ordained that after a prefixed day set downe in the said Decree, they should not enioy any other priuiledge or immunitie, then anie other strangers in the said Citie: which assoone as her Maiestie and her hono-rable Counsell vnderstood, they requited the Hanses with a like Decree, which yet was suspéded til the 25. of Iuly. **1579.** at which time her Maiestie, not receiuing any satisfaction at the Hanses hands, but to the contrarie vnderstáding, that the said Hanses, at an Assembly at *Lunenburgh*, the second of No-uember **1579.** had set forth an Edict for the leuying of 7¾ vpon the hundred of all goods brought by Englishmen into their territories, or carried out of the same: Her Highnesse vp-pon this occasion commanded the like decree to be made, for the taking of the like summe vpon the goods of the Han-ses, and in this estate the matter stood on both parts, till that by a petition put vp by the Alderman of the Steelyard this last decree of 7¾ vpon the 100. was suspended for foure mo-neths: but the first, because it depended vpon the restraint of Trade of her Maiesties subiects, the Lords of the Councell thought not good to suspend, or reuoke the same, til the contents thereof were satisfied, and fulfilled.

And thus I haue briefly and truely set downe what hath passed, and in what state at this day the whole controuersie betweene her Maiestie, and the *Hanses* standeth: by the discourse whereof I doubt not, but it plainly appeareth, that (as aforesaid)the *Hanses* haue no iust or lawfull cause to complaine, for that they haue themselues beene the cause of all that happened. For first, the resuming of their Priuiledges in the dayes of King *Edward*, proceeded of this, that they freed and coloured mens goods that were none of their societie, and for other causes aboue rehearsed. Secondly, when as Queene *Marie* had reuoked that, which had bene done by her brother, she her selfe at length reuoked the said Reuocation, for that the *Hanses* had broken promise with her, in continuing an vnlawfull trade in the low Countries, whereby she lost in her Customes within the space of eleuen moneths, more then 9360 pound sterling, besides the dammage sustained by her subiects in their trade, and when as she offered a meeting for the deciding of all controuersies: the *Hanses* vtterly refused the same, and would none of it. Thirdly, her Maiestie that now is, when she came first to the Crowne, commanded that the *Hanses* should be vsed as well (yea in some points better) then her owne subiects, but they in recompence of this fauour, not prouoked with any new occasion, commanded that the exercise and trade of Merchandise graunted to her Highnesse subiects by the Hamburgers, *cum clausula perpetuitatis* shuld be broken off, & disanulled: & afterward when her Ma^{tie} required a reformation of this their Decree, they in steed thereof imposed that exaction of theirs of seuen and three quarters vpon the hundred: And so with their new impositions, their refusing of a meeting, and Conference in England, their abusing of their libertie in the low Countries, by doing manie things to the preiudice of her Maiestie and subiects, by diminishing the reuenewes of the Crowne, by colouring other mens goods, vnder the pretence of their Priuiledges, they were finally

*The Hanses them selues are the cause of the restraint of their priuiledges in England.*

nally depriued of their liberties, and immunities at the pleasure of her Highnesse, yet alwayes were more friendly vsed,
then any other the subiects of the Princes in amitie & league
with her Maiestie, for the which they neuer shewed any
sparke of thankfulnesse, but haue from time to time vniustly
accused her Highnes to forreigne princes and States, her Maiesties louing friendes and confederates, and to this day with
much clamorousnes and importunacie leaue not off to doe
the same without respect to the person and qualitie of so
excellent & gracious a Princesse, & doing that which is farre
vnbeseeming their State and condition, but if they thinke
to get any thing hereby in the ende, they are much deceiued
in mine opinion, their way to speed is to proceed *cum preca-
tione & supplicatione*, and not by the way of force and com-
pulsion : *Magnorum siquidem Principum & Regum heroicis
animis natura videtur insitum, quod flecti, & duci, non cogi velint.*

The third cause whereupon the foresaid Mandate of the
Emperours is grounded, is, *The Monopolie vsed* (as is said) by
the *Marchants Aduenturers*: which to be a false and iniurious
slander, and surmize, needeth no other demonstration, then
the true sence and definition of the word *Monopolie* it selfe :
*Quum Monopolium sit quando vnus solus aliquod genus merca-
tura vniuersum emit, vt solus suo arbitrio vendat. Monopolie* is,
when one man alone buyeth vp all that is to bee got of one
kinde of merchandise, to the end that he alone may sell at his
owne lust and pleasure. Which wel considered, hath no com-
munion or agreement with the trade & practise of the Companie of M.M. Aduenturers, and townes where the said companie haue resided, or are resident in at this day, doe knowe
and can witnesse, that those of the said Companie haue vsed,
and doe vse an honest, vpright and lawfull trade *Emptionis,
Venditionis, & Permutationis* : which by all lawe is permitted,
*vita enim nostra sine contractibus & commercijs subsistere ne-
quit*, not onely with Cloth, but also with all kinde of wares,
and Merchandise, so that whatsoeuer is free and at libertie
to buy and sell, the same by no reason or right construction

*Defense of the
M.M. Aduentu-
rers against the
Hanses slander
of Monopolie.*

N 3      can

can be accompted a *Monopolie*: neither haue the Adventurers
the sole transporte, and trade inwardes, and outwardes of
English Cloth, and other Wares, but it is well knowen, and
notorious, that all the Members of the *Hanses*, & not onely
they, but also all the subiects of Vpper, and Low Germanie,
and all other straungers in league, & amitie with the Crowne
of England, may, and doe at their libertie and pleasure, buye,
and carry out of the Realme all sortes of Cloth, and English
wares, and may, and doe bring in, and sell their own countrie
commodities without empeachment, or hinderance, pay-
ing such dewties, and customes, as they ought to pay: besides there are diuerse other Companies of Merchantes, who
are priviledged to transporte Cloth, &c. out of the lande into
forreigne partes, and Cuntries, as well as the Companie of M.
M. Adventurers, which they doe in great quantitie. Moreouer, the Companie of M. M Adventurers hath no banke, nor
common stocke, nor common Factour to buye, or sell for
the whole Companie, but euery man tradeth a-part and par-
ticularlie with his owne stocke, and with his owne Factour, or
seruaunt: wherevpon it necessarilie followeth, that forasmuch
as the M. M. Aduenturers haue not (as aforesaid) the sole dealing, and traffike alone in their own hands, either in Englande
or on the other side the seas, and that *Monopoly definitio cum*
*suo definito* in the least parte agreeth not, the said companie by
no sound reason, or argument can be charged to bee anie
such Monopoliers, or priuat gain, & lucre seekers, as the *Han-*
*ses* would make the world beleeue they are, neither is it to be
thought, that by the said M. M. Aduenturers the said *Hanses*
are brought to such apparant losse, and hinderaunce, as by
their complaintes they beare the Emperour, and States of the
Empire in hand. Concerning that, which they alleadge, that
the said companie haue their Gouernement, and Officers,
keepe Courtes, and Assemblies, make lawes, impose mulctes
and penalties, and shippe at set times, and with appointed
Fleetes, out of which they would infer a Monopolie: It needeth none other answer, then I haue alreadie made in this treatise, wherein is truelie and plainly declared the practise, and
maner of the Companie of M. M. Aduenturers in al the aboue
said

faide pointes, and withall ſhewed the good, that commeth to
the State, and common Wealth thereby, and how farre it is
out of the compaſſe of *Monopolie*: A fault not only forbidden,
but alſo worthilie to be puniſhed in all well gouerned common wealthes, *Imo honeſtorum Principum ſubditis indignum:*
Beſides, it is more then ſtrange, that the *Hanſes* haue the face
to códemne that in others, as vnlawful, & Monopoliſh, which
themſelues both in Englande, and euery where elſe, where
they now haue, or haue had their Reſidence, or Counters có-
tinually practiſed: for who knoweth not, that they had their
Aldermen, or Conſuls, Treaſurers, Secretaries, Aſſiſtentes, &
other officers, & keepe their meetinges, Courtes, & Aſſem-
blies, & vſed Marchants law amóg themſelues? And if it were
lawfull, & free for thē ſo to doe, why may it not be as lawfull,
& free for the M.M. Adventurers to doe the like? But (ſay the
Hanſes) the M.M. Adventurers in their Courtes doe ſet the
prices of their own wares, & of other mens, ordayning not to
ſell or buye otherwiſe, or at other rates, or prices, which is
plaine *Monopolie*, this how true it is, I appeale to the conſcien-
ces of the verie *Hanſes* themſelues, & of all other Merchants,
with whom the ſaid Companie doe deale, whether this be a
trueth yea, or no. Beſides, I may boldlie, & with a good con-
ſcience affirme, that neither I in all the time of my ſeruice, neither the oldeſt man liuing in the ſaide Companie, can ſaye,
that euer it was knowen, or heard that any ſuch matter of ſetting price was once mentioned in any Court, or aſſemblie of
the ſaid Companie: neither in deed was there euer any ſuch
matter, but euery mā rather ſtudieth to keep his feat & trade
as ſecrete to himſelfe as he can, for feare of his fellow, leaſt being eſpied, it might be taken out of his handes, & further, it is a
thing abhorred, & condemned by the lawes of the Realme, &
therefore if the Companie of M.M. Aduenturers could euer
haue been iuſtlie accuſed of the ſaid crime, they ſhould not
haue eſcaped ſo long without deſerued puniſhment: laſtlie,
the verie ſtate, and policie of the ſaid Companie, cannot a-
bide or brooke anie Monopolie, as being directlie, and
*ex diametro* contrarie, and an ouerthrow to that Oeconomie, ſo carefully prouided for, and preſerued by the good
lawes,

lawes, and orders of the said Companie : whereby there is a
distribution of the benefites, and Commodities of the Company to all the members of the same, so much, as is possible
with great prouidence, and equitie ordained, so that euery
man that will or is able, may participate thereof so farre, as
they will extend: Whereas if it were otherwise, the meaner
sort should not be able to liue by the richer: for these in short
time would with their great purses and meanes drawe all the
trade inwardes and outwardes into their owne hands, and as
vpon the Bankers in some places) all mens credites should
depend vpon their sleeues, as hauing power to giue credite
to whome they list, to sell or keepe vp their wares, at their
pleasure, and to rule the markets as they thinke good: whereby it would come to passe, that a fewe shall gaine and growe
mightie & exceeding wealthy, and all the rest shall haue nothing to doe, and in short time be brought to extreame mise-
rie and pouertie: but the gouerned trade of the said Companie is here in the way, so that you see how farre it is frō trueth,
or likelihood of trueth, which is obiected against the Companie of M. M. Aduenturers on this behalfe, as beeing rather
an vtter enemie then a friend, or liker of that greedy or inordinate course: as appeareth partly by that abouesaid, & more
euidently, as well by the testimonie of strangers of diuers nations, as also by the Attestations, vnder the seales of great and
famous Cities (whereof some are of the *Hanses* themselues)
which I haue set downe not onely for the credite, commendation and iustifying of the said Company, but withall for the
more manifestation of the trueth of that which hath beene a-
bouesaid. And first the Senate of *Hambrough*, at such time as
they caused to be denounced to the company the expiration
of their priuiledges, did in their Insinuation the ninetenth of
Iuly 1577. expressely put these words. *Quæ quidem Denuncia-*
*tio non eo animo fit, quod Societas Mercatorum, quæ se honestè*
*in hac Ciuitate gessit, & integritate sua bonorum virorum bene-*
*uolentiam meretur, Senatui nostra molesta, & grauis sit, verum*
*solummodò vt pactis satisfiat:* And afterwards, *Etenim si inclita*
*Societas Mercatorum florentissimi Regni Angliæ diutius in hac*

*Ciui-*

*Testimonie of*
*strangers and*
*whole Cities on*
*the companies be-*
*halfe against the*
*slander of Mono-*
*polie.*

*Ciuitate commorare, mercaturam exercere, & hoc nomine noua*
*pacta posteaquam priora expirarunt cum spectabili Senatu inire in*
*animo habeat, Senatui officio suo & æquitati non deerit.* Wherby
it appeereth in what eltimation the faid Senat held the Companie of Merchantes Adventurers, in that they not only commended them for their honeſt cariage, and integritie, but alſo
offer the further fauour, & entertainement in their Citie after
the ending of the former priuiledges, which were agreed vpon but for ten yeares, yet with this Addition, *Quod elapſis ſu-*
*pradictis annis conceſsio dictorum Priuilegiorum renouaretur, &*
*continuaretur in infinitum, ſi interim non caderet in Ciuitatis ſuæ*
*damnum, vel diſpendium:* Now that the faid Citie receiued neither loſſe nor damage by the Cōpanie of Merchants Aduenturers, the aboue written words of honeſt cariage, and integritie, proceeding frō the Magiſtrates themſelues in the ſame
Citie doe ſufficientlie beare witnes, and fince that time alſo
more perticularlie the faid Senate of *Hambroughe* doeth
touche that point of *Monopoly* in a letter writē to the Gouernour and Generalitie of the faid Companie in Auguſt 1586.
wherein they ſay, that although they cannot denie, but that
there were complaintes made vnder that name of *Monopolie*
to the Emperour, and Princes Electours, *tamen noſtra cum ſuf-*
*fragatione, & approbatione eaſdem inſtitutas eſſe cōſtanter nega-*
*mus: Ideoφ, quum hæ Actiones ex aliorum potius ſuffragijs, quàm*
*ex noſtra voluntate, & arbitrio dependeant, non dubitamus Mag-*
*nificentias, & Dominationes veſtras diuerſorum diſcrepàntes in-*
*tentiones, & ſententias maturiore iudicio diſcuſſuros:* ſo that in this
point a man may ſee they agreed not with the reſt of their fellowes whoſe doings they diſclaime as hauing no voice or allowance of theirs. Likewife the late L. *Egdard,* Earle of *Eaſt-*
*friſeland* in a letter by him writē in anſwer of a Mandate from
the Emperour, the 26. of July 1580. concerning the aboue
faid ſlander of *Monopolie,* & monopoliſh trade vſed in *Emb-*
*dē* by the Engliſh, hath theſe words: *Now whatſoeuer is free to*
*al men, & forbidden to none, & when as this tēdeth not to the pri-*
*uate cōmodity of one, or of ſome few ſingular perſons, nor goeth vpō*
*any one ſort of wares,* as hē had ſhewed that the trade of M.M.

O                    Ad-

Adventurers did not *this by a Monopolie, or Monopolish trade, that referre I most humbly to your Maiesties consideration, be-side the Title of Monopolies in the lawe declareth, whether it be so yea, or no:it was therefore neuer my meaning or thought to graunt vnto the English, or any other such Monopolish trade, but such, as the law permitteth to al men:and in very deed there is no such mo-nopolish trade vsed at Embden, and therein I referre my self to any iust proofe, and all both straungers, and others, which vnderstande these doings, and can herein witnes the same with mee:* This testi-monie of the Earles, the Senat of the town of *Embden,* confir-med by an Attestation vnder their common seale, bearing date the 28. of Iuly 1582. the true copie whereof, & of other the like vnder the seals of the cities of *Antwerpe, Middelburgh* and *Stade,* I haue set downe at the ende of this Treatise, wher-by I doubt not, but all the world may perceiue that the Impu-tation of *Monopolie* to the companie of M. M. Adventurers, is but a malicious, iniurious, and altogether false slaunder, de-uised by the *Hanses,* (as I said before) to draw the Emperour, and Princes of Germanie, to assist them in the obtaining of their vniust pretences, and vnreasonable demaunds in Eng-land, to the dishonor of her Maiestie, and hurt of the whole State, as much as in them lyeth, which God defend that they should haue their willes in. Lastlie, to knit vp this point, I will adde herevnto as a golden *Corronis* of all that hath been said, the iudgment of her Highnes our most gracious Soueraigne, and the true defence of the saide Companie in certaine her Maiesties letters to the Emperour, and diuerse of the Princes of Germanie and namelie in one to the Emperour written in Noueber 1595. the eight of the said Moneth, in these words: *Monopolium porrò de quo Hanseatici subditos nostros crimina-tur, calumniæ potius, quam veræ accusationis rationem præ se ferre videtur, ab ipsis enim Imperij subditis, qui Londini resident, ailigê-ter inquiri iussimus, si quid solidi de iniquis subditorum nostrorum negotiandi rationibus referre possent: illi verò ingenué responde-runt se nihil ea de re in commissis habere acturos; tamen se quam-primum per literas cum suis Maioribus, quumque demùm quid responsi acciperent, id totum fideliter relaturos: quæstionem prate-*
rea

*rea ea de re cum subditis nostris institui mandauimus, Illi verò*
*authenticis scriptis edocent, negotiandi ipsorum rationes à plurimis*
*ciuitatibus in Belgio, Prussia, atque alibi vti honestissimas probari,*
*atque quum duæ Imperij Ciuitates sint, quæ cum nostris maximè*
*negotiantur, Lubeca, & Haburgum, illarum altera publicis lite-*
*ris, vt nostri ostendunt, testata est, ipsorum Negotiationem ab om-*
*ni Monopolij suspicione vacuã esse, seq̃, illius obiectæ criminationis*
*participes nunquam fuisse: vbi verò Hanseaticorũ institores plura*
*ea de re ex Dominorum suorum expectata in scriptis cõmissione*
*opposuerint, se quoq; pluribus in scriptis responsuros humiliter ob-*
*tulerunt .* This whole letter, for that it contayneth matter
woorthie the knowledge concerning the *Hanses,* I haue added vnto the ende of this Treatise: Her said Maiestie in another letter to the Emperor, dated the 20 of December 1597
sent by Maister *Iohn Wrothe,* after her Highnes had complay-
ned of the vnorderlie setting foorth & publishing of the Emperors Mandate for the reasons in the said letter at large set
down, hath these words following: *Quæ si paulò attentiùs*
*Maiestas vestra ratione animoq̃, ponderasset, & ea quæ literis no-*
*stris anno 1595. menseque Nouẽbri conscriptis sunt comprehensa*
*collatione cum vestris literis mense Iulij facta, diligentiùs consi-*
*derasset ( de quibus literis vel factiosorum hominum machinationi-*
*bus vos cælatos esse, vel à quibusdam ex ijs, qui vestræ Maiestati*
*sunt à Cõsilijs non optima fide vobiscum actũ esse magnopere suspi-*
*camur ) nobis certè persuassissimum est, vos hanc rationem tam*
*iniquã Edicti contra nos, subditosque nostros vestro Imperio haud-*
*quaquam subiectos, promulgandi nunquam fuisse suscepturos, sed*
*potius repudiaturos has commentitias Hanseaticorum querelas:*
*quibus quidem præter eorum merita par atque eadem libertas in*
*Mercaturis apud nos faciendis, quæ nostris hominibus conceditur*
*oblata est: denique facturos fuisse, vt actiones nostræ remotis par-*
*tium studijs, fictisque delationibus ad rationis normã & æquitatis,*
*ac iustitiæ ponderibus examinaretur .* And in letters at the same
time written to the Princes of Germanie and sent by the said
M. *Wroth,* & M. *Stephen Lesure,* to wit, to the Administra-
tor of *Saxonie* to the *Palsgraue* vpon the Rhine, the Elector of
*Mentz,* & diuers others, her Maiestie writeth in these words:

*Eodem porrò Edicto nonnulla in priscam quandam subditorum no-*
*strorū Societatem (quam Adventurariorum vocant) obiecta com-*
*memorantur, atque ex ijsdem proscriptionis veluti sententia infer-*
*tur, qua & ex Imperij finibus discedere, atque ab omni intra eos-*
*dem emendi ac vendendi vsu abstinere iubentur, qua quidem res*
*admiratione digna videtur, maximè cùm literis nostris ad Impera-*
*torē mense Nouēbri, An. 1595. à Comitijs quæ Ratisbonæ 94. ha-*
*bebantur datis ad singula Edicto hoc repetita abunde responsum,*
*ac firmissimis rerū momentis satisfactū fuerit, quo sanè credendum*
*nobis erat Cæsareā Maiest. biennium penè silentio interposito ratio-*
*nibus à nobis allatis acquieuisse. Quod si quid adhuc dubij superesse*
*visum fuisset, & iustitia, & regiæ nostræ dignitatis ratio, quā sub di-*
*uino numine absolutā gerimus, pro amicitia saltē nostra quā sanctè*
*hactenus cū Imperio coluimus, aut per literas per internūciū aliquē*
*nobis exponendum illud postulasset. Nunc verò hunc in modum sub*
*silentio ex improuiso, etiā Typis exposuisse quæ ad nostrā iniuriam*
*(ipsa quoque in subditos nostros. iustitia violata) faciunt, indecorum*
*omnino fuisse arbitramur: omnium enim opinione iniquum meritò*
*habēdum viros probos nunquā auditos, aut vocatos ex maleuolorū*
*obiectis calumnijs, nec probatis, & ne quidem ritè examinatis pro-*
*scriptionis sententia, etiam contra ipsam sacri Imperij libertatem*
*mulctasse.* Thus you see what the opinion of her Maiestie & of
others hath beene of the Companie of the M. M. Aduenturers touching Monopoly, whereof they are slandered by the
*Hanses,* which I doubt not is sufficient though not possibly to
stop the mouthes of the said *Hanses,* yet to conuince them of
vntruth, and malicious forgery on that behalfe.

## That the maintenance of the Fellowship of Merchants Ad-uenturers hath beene and is for the honour and seruice of the Prince and State at home and abroad.

LL that which hath bin afore at large set downe,
tēdeth in effect to the proof of this point, as if it
wold please the diligent Reader to remember
the same, and lay it together, would be soone
perceiued. For whereas I haue said, & shewed
that

that the Merchants Aduenturers, as subiects of this noble Realme, haue procured at the hands of forreigne Princes and States many ample, and beneficiall Iurisdictions, Priuiledges, Liberties, exemptions and immunities, by vertue whereof they haue erected a good and conuenient gouernment, for the rule and ordering of themselues, and their Trade, & exercise ciuill iurisdiction beyond the seas: that the said Merchants Aduenturers are a meanes of the preseruation of the amitie and league betweene this land, and the said forreigne Princes and States, that they aduaunce the price, and vent of our countrie Commodities, and bring in forreigne wares good cheape, that they are a maintenance of the Nauigation and encrease of the customs at home, who seeth not, & confesseth that all these things are to the high honor of the Prince, and notable seruice of the state and common wealth? Besides all this, some of the Princes of this land haue known so well, how to vse this Company, and to make their vttermost benefite of them, that besides that the said Companie haue at sundrie times vpon vrgent occasions giuen their credits for the lones of great summes of money beyond the seas, for the seruice of the State, diuerse of the Gouernours, and others of the said Companie, haue in particular not beene wanting, according to their dutie, to do their Prince good, and commendable seruice manie times in the affaires of the State. Further, at the change of Princes, and receiuing in of new, at Triumphs for victories, and Coronations, the said Companie haue not forgot the honour of their Prince and Countrie, but haue spent and laid out great summes of money this way, so that at some one Princes receiuing in, they haue consumed aboue two thousand French Crownes in shewes or triumphall Arches, and namely, of the late King *Philip* of Spaine, at his entrie into the Citie of *Antwerpe* in September 1549. at such time, as his father the Emperour *Charles* the fifth, transferred vnto him all his Seignories, and States in the lowe Countries: besides, that Maister *Iohn Sturgeon*, at that time Gouernour of the Company was at the receiuing in of the said Prince, accompanied with thirtie Merchants of the Companie on horse-

backe,

back al in a liuerie of purple veluet in graine coats, and paned
hofe, embroidered full of filuer waues, like the waues of the
fea : their Dublets, and drawing out of their hofe purple fat-
tin, their Hats of purple veluet with golde bands, faire brou-
ches, and white feathers : and each of them a chaine of gold
about his necke of great value : buskins of purple veluet: their
Rapiers, Daggers, Spurres, Stirrops, and Bridles all gilt : the
furniture of their horfes was of purple veluet, Saddles and
trappings, &c. embroidered with gold and greene filke, and
white and greene feathers on their horfe heads: they were
attended with threefcore Lackeyes, apparrelled in white veluet ierkins cut, imbroidered with filuer twift, greene fatten
Dublets, with hofe and buskins of the fame, purple veluet
Caps and greene feathers: behind them rode the abouefaid
Gouernour vpon a white Englifh gelding, in a long purple
veluet gowne, lined with purple fatten : a blacke veluet coat,
and cappe with a faire brouch therein, and a chaine of gold a-
bout his necke : his Dublet and Hofe, with the trappings of
his Horfe were, as the other of his Company wore, he was attended on by fixe Lackies on foote, and three Pages on
horfebacke, apparelled as aforefaid. In which their doing,
they fhewed themfelues for the honour of their Prince and
Countrie, nothing inferiour to the Merchants of other nations, namely the Germans, Eafterlings, Italians, Spaniards, and
Portugals, and furmounting fome of them in coftly apparel,
furniture of themfelues and their horfes, and in other preparation, to entertaine the faid Prince, whereby they wan great
honour, and commendation to themfelues, and the whole
Englifh name. To fay nothing of the late Duke of *Alanfons*
entertainment into the faid Citie of *Antwerpe* in the yeare
1581. at which time Maifter *Chriftopher Hoddefdon* then, and
now Gouernour, receiued the faid Duke with fourefcore
Merchants of the Companie, all on horfeback in verie feemly
and decent fort, apparelled in blacke veluet, and moft of them
with chaines of gold about their necks: for the which the faid
Gouernour & Companie receiued thankes and commendations from her Maieftie and the Lords of the Councel, wher-

of

of some were beholders of that abouesaid, and made honourable report thereof vnto her Highnesse at their return home. In deedes of Pietie, and Charitie they haue not also beene wanting, as well appeareth by the founding of Chappels in old time at *Bridges* and *Middelburgh* : and since, in maintaining the exercise of Religion amongst them in all the places of their residence hetherto, yea euen amóg those, who could not well away with the same : as also by their Christianlike care, and prouision for the poore, the comfort whereof many a distressed person, souldiers, and mariners &c. of our nation haue found, and daily find : besides, their liberalitie is knowne to a great manie, who heretofore haue tatted the same, especially those, who haue, & do receiue yearly pésions from thé, partly in remembrance, and gratification of passed seruice, and partly for their better reliefe, maintenance, and sustentation in their old dayes as also in learning and otherwise: hereunto may be added the great, and continuall charges, which from time to time they haue beene at, and still are in these troublesome times, through the manifold disturbance, remouing, and alteration of the Trade about the procuring of new Priuiledges, and residence for the better vent, and vtterance of the Commodities of the realme, and maintenance of the Commerce, and traffike in forreigne parts. And when for the defence of the Realme, shippes haue beene to bee made out, it hath cost them notable summes of money, as by their accounts thereof doth appeare : all which could not haue bin done, but by men vnited into a Societie or compánie, as wold be too too euident, if once all were set at libertie, as some would haue it : for then it would in few yeares come to passe, that we should neither haue priuiledge, nor iurisdiction abroad, the friendship, and kind of vsage of our neighbours would waxe cold, and faint, yea wee should go to the walles, be wróged & exacted vpon euery where, our Countrie commodities would grow vile, or come into the hands, and managing of strangers, at whose curtesie also, or at least of a few Cormorants of our own nation, we should stand, for that we haue need of from abroad: by meanes whereof the incomes

and

and Customes of the Prince, would be sore diminished, and
the Nauigation decayed: and lastlie, if there were occasion
either at home of anie thing of importance to be done on the
suddaine for the defence of the Realme, the extraordinarie
helpe of the M.M. Adventurers would bee wanting, and in
forreigne partes, if there were neede, either of money, or o-
ther prouision for the seruice of the Prince, and State, no man
would be founde, and so neither credite, nor meanes would
be founde or had to serue the turne withall, neither any man
to doe anie thing for the honour of the Prince, and Countrie
howsoeuer necessarie, or vrgent the occasion may be, either
generall, or particular: all which I doubt not will be well considered of, and waighed by her Excellent Maiestie, and those
which vnder her Highnes haue the ordering, and gouernement of the affaires, and state of this noble Realm, and so the
common wealth may prosper, & encrease in honour, & flou-
rishing estate, & that those, which trauaile, and take paines to
this ende, and haue from time to time bene found profitable
members, may be cherished, and maintained in their well
doing, and encouraged to proceede, by vouchsafing them
gratious countenance, and favourable ayde, and assistance in
their causes, and by vpholding them in the full and quiet frui-
tion, and vse of their Priuiledges, Charters, and Rightes giue
heeretofore with so good consideration, and hetherto continued to the high Honour of her Maiestie, and the generall
good of this Realme, as I hope in this treatise to haue plainly,
and euidentlie prooued, to the reasonable satisfactiō of al that
loue not nouelties, or haue no outladish appetites: especiallie
of those in honorable, and eminent place, for whose information principallie I vndertooke this labour, humbly praying
that it may be well accepted, and bring foorth such good, as
is thereby meant vnto her Roiall Maiestie, and the whole
lande with all the members thereof, the continuall happines,
and prosperitie wherof the Almightie graunt, by whom Princes raigne, & without whome nothing is happie, or perdura-
ble. And you true hearted Marchantes Advēturers, for whose
sake I haue writen This treatise, faint not in your orderlie, and
hetherto

hetherto wel continued courfe vnder the fauor & protection
of fo excellent & gratious a Princeffe, which you haue oftentimes proued, & feen, and by the aid and direction of fo Honorable and wife a Councell, as that of her Ma^ties, of whom
you may be wel affured, to receiue all neceffarie and reafona-
ble affiftance in your honeft and commendable exercife and
feate of Merchandife, maintaine the credite & honour which
you haue gotten abroad, continue in well doing, keepe you
to your ancient orders, and Policie: Preferue vnion and con-
cord amongft you diligently and carefully, *& valeant qui dif-*
*fidium inter vos volunt,* note them not withftanding, and looke
vnto them betymes, for they are daungerous perfons, louers
of them felues, and enemies to your good, and the welfare
of your Societie, wherein they & the *Hanfes* iumpe together
and agree: for neith er the one, nor the other would haue you
to be a Copanie for that is in their way, & reftrained the ones
inordinate gourmandife, and thirft after priuate lucre, onely
regardinge the time prefent, and nothing at all the pofteritie
(which is a peftilet & pernicious humor in al comon wealths)
and keepeth the other from praying vpon the comon wealth
of this Realme, & hauing their will of the ftate: as for the faide
*Hanfes* flaunderous complaintes, and accufations of *Monopo-*
*lie* forged without ground of trueth, it fhalbe for your credite
to anfwere, where they fhalbe afhamed of their doinges, and
at length blufh, *vendere tam vanos circum Palatia fumos:* which
you may eafilie do, and without any great charge: and for the
*Hanfes* them felues neither they, nor their means are fo great,
that the State need greatlie to fear them, for if we wil but co-
fider the caufes, that made them of eftimation, and accompt
in olde time, namely, the multitude of their fhipping, and fea
trade whereby they ftored al Countries with the Eafterne comodities, and ferued Princes turnes in time of warre, and of
vfe of fhipping : wee fhall finde that they haue in a manner
loft both the one and the other long agoe in comparifon of
that it hath been, and is now at this day with them: And if her
Maieftie fhould forbid all trade into Spaine after the example
of other Princes they would in fhort time be quitt of the reft.

for that trade is their chiefett support at this inftant, and might be taken frõ them: if it fo were thought meet vnto her Highnes, and the Lords; and others of her Honorable Councel: Befides of the two and feueptie confederate *Hanfe* Townes, fo much fpoken, and vaunted of, what remaineth almoft, but the reperte, and thofe which remaine, & appeare by their Deputies whẽ there is anie affemblie, are they of one minde? or are they able, but with much adoe, to bring vp the charges and contributious neceffarie, & incident for the defence, and maintenance of their league, Priuiledges, & trade in foreigne partes, and at home? furely no: fo that it appeareth, that they are not the men they haue been, and therefore although their ftomacks, & malice no doubt be bigge enough, yet we need not much to regard, what they can do, for moft of their teeth are out, & the remayner are but loofe, & fcattred: much better therfore were it for them, to feeke the recouery of her Maiefties fauor, and grace by fome other more decent courfe, and meanes, then they haue of late practifed, *Precatio & fupplicatio* were fitter for them, and would become them better, as I faid before, let them remẽber the difficulties, which fome of the *Hanfe* townes are already brought into by their neighbor Princes, & what yet hangeth ouer fome other of their heads, for the preuenting or remoouing of the like, whereof the verie opinion of the good will, and friendfhip of her Highneffe would not bee a little auailable, and may profite much hereafter: Wherefore like wife men, knowing their fault, and errour, let them fhape another courfe, for this, which they hetherto haue runne, will not bring them there where they would faigne be: And when all is done, and that they haue fpent their monie and wearied the world with their importunate complaintes, and out-cryes do they thinke that they fhal recouer their priuiledges in Englande by forcing her Maieftie, or the State? I fuppofe they are not fo fenfeles. As for the trade in Cloth out of England, which they fo much contẽd for, I am of opinion if the matter were wel examined, that the riotoufneffe, and vnfaithfull dealing of their feruants, and factors, the aduenture of the fea, and charges, when they

ſhipfhipped, and held the Steelyard at London confidered, they did more profite by buying of the Merchants Aduenturers at *Embden*, and *Hamburgh*, efpecially the Merchants of *Hamburgh*, then by fetching of Cloth themfelues out of England. But let that be, as it may be, I muft confeffe, that the ancient friendfhip, and Commerce between the Realme of England and the *Hanfes* (howfoeuer they be now decayed) ought not altogether to be forgotten, that fo by fome good & indifferent meanes and agreement, the Trade & Amitie betweene the two moft noble Dutch, & Englifh nations might be made firme & ftable, & the ancient & friendly neighborhood confirmed againft all humane changes and chaunces, which are vncertaine and variable : yet fo, that ftrangers be not preferred before the Naturall borne fubiect, who at all times is and muft be ready to ferue his Prince & country with his perfon and goods at home, and abroad, when ftrangers, and ftrange help wilbe far off, and to feeke : And therefore the demaund of the *Hanfes* in this behalfe is very abfurd, and vnreafonable, *Nam fitientibus noftris agris alienos irrigare, ftultum effe Leges ducunt, & ordinatam Charitatem incipere à feipfo, etiam Theologi admittunt*: wherewith I will conclude this *Treatife*, hoping that therein I haue fufficientlie declared, and made known that, which I tooke vpon me at the beginning, namelie: *The Commodities of a well ordered Trade*, fuch as I doubt not, I haue proued that of the Societie or Companie of M.M. Adventurers to bee, and the *Neceffaries of the faid Societie* in this florifhing *State*.

*Quem Deus incolumem feruet, faxitq, perennem,*
That fo the memebers, and parts thereof may continually, and dayly more and more profper, and
grow vp in the fame, to the honor of
God, their Prince and
Countrie.

# A COPIE OF A LETTER FROM

*her Maiestie in answer of a letter receiued from the Empe-*
*rour in high Dutch, wherof the Mandate maketh*
*mention, but much differing from the*
*contents of this Copie.*

*LIZABETHA Dei gratia Angliæ,*
*Franciæ, & Hiberniæ Regina, fidei defensor,*
*&c. Sereniſsimo Principi ac Domino, Domi-*
*no RODOLPHO, Romanorum E-*
*lecto Imperatori ſemper Auguſto: Regi*
*Hungariæ, Bohemiæ, Dalmatiæ & Slaa-*
*niæ: Archiduci Auſtriæ: Duci Burgundiæ,*
*Styriæ, Carinthiæ & Wirtinbergæ: Comiti Tyrollis, &c. Fra-*
*tri & Conſanguineo noſtro chariſsimo: Salutem rerumque opta-*
*tiſsimarum fœlicisſmū incrementum.*

 *Sereniſsime Princeps, Frater & Conſanguinee chariſsi-*
*me, Literæ Serenitatis veſtræ decimo quinto Iulÿ data, & illæ*
*quidem Germanice conscriptæ, quod ſane primo aſpectu, cum id*
*genus idiomatis hactenus inter nos haud vſitatum ſit, dubitationem*
*an cōmentitiæ eſſent non leuem ingeſsit) ſub finem Octobris redditæ*
*nobis fuerunt, quas quidem ex ſubiecta materia ad Hanſeatico-*
*rum inſtantiam editas animaduertimus: . Illi vero dum obſoleta*
*quædam Priuilegia in Regno noſtro ſibi ipſi vendicare perperam*
*deereuiſſent An. octuageſimo ſecundo in Imperialibus comitÿs Au-*
*guſtæ Vindelicorum habitis, Mandatum (vt hiſce ſerenitatis veſtræ*
*literis habetur) de communibus Imperÿ ac Dominiorum noſtrorū*
*commercÿs perturbandis extorſerunt: & iam nuper anno nonageſi-*
*mo quarto in Deputatorum conuentu Ratisboniæ, de ipſorum dam-*
*nis Mari per Thalaſſos noſtros (vt queruntur) illatis, denique*
*Mercatorum noſtrorum in Imperio negotiandi rationibus*
*(quas illi odioſa appellatione Monopolia vocitant) nonnullis alle-*
*gatis & deductis, Mandati illius Auguſtani vim atque executio-*
*nem poſtularunt. Hac occaſione Serenitas veſtra pro mutua Ami-*
*citia noſtra (quam amantiſsmæ Sororis affectu libenter amplecti-*
*mur) ſcribendum hoc tempore duxit; noſq; hiſce ſuis amicè horta-*
*tur,*

tur, vt de eiusmodi malorum remedijs cogitemus, quibus sine que-
relis imposito, omnia in florentissimo Amicitiæ statu conseruentur.

Eo certé animo in Serenitatem vestrâ totumǫ, ipsius Imperium
semper fuimus, vt arctissimæ Amicitiæ iura cum eadem perpetuò
tueri, atque inuiolatè colere statuerimus; quam quidem animi nostri propensionem, vti pro re nata sæpiùs testatissimam reddere hactenus studuimus, ita deinceps mutui amoris nostri officijs nunquã
deerimus. Ad Hanseaticorum querelas quod attinet, commu-
nes querelarum rationes subire illas necesse est: vt nempè quã mi-
niùs rectè institutæ reperiantur, seipsis concidant. Atqui de me-
moratis Priuilegijs sæpe iam aliàs responsum est: illa ipsa ante Inau-
gurationem nostram collapsa, atque ex allegatis & probatis publico
ac summo Regni nostri Iudicio (à quo nullum Appellationis forum
agnoscitur) penitus euersa atque abolita fuisse. Nos verò alia nonnulla vt temporum rationes ferebant, aliquamdiu Hanseaticis
côcessimus; donec ipsi peculiari ipsorum decreto, subditos nostros
tum Hamburgæ cum laude residentes, nulla dignitatis nec amicitiæ
nostræ ratione habita, nulla ex causa, nobisǫ omnino non præmonitis
temerè exturbarent. Post aliquanto cùm à Serenitate vestrâ com-
mẽdatitias in fauorem illorum accepissemus, ad easdem omninò
apud nos negotiandi rationes, quibus ipsi nostri subditi vtuntur,
illis in gratiam Serenitatis vestræ concedendas, satis nos inclinatas
sæpe ostẽdimus; nihil tamen illi eo in genere hactenus à nobis petie-
runt. Nunc igitur Serenitas vestra cui Deus optimus maximus
populos subiecit, multo rerum vsu edocta quænam sint sceptra te-
nendi rationes, ipsa secum perpendat, an iis aures præbendæ sint, qui
vetusta priuilegia Iuris ordine semel abiudicata, & eam olim penitus deleta, quæ mutati ab priscis temporum atque hominum
mores non ferunt, cineribus suscitare multa importunitate sata-
gunt? Quis enim esset rerumpub. status, si quæ iam olim iustis de
caussis antiquata oportuit, ad preces cuiuspiam in vsum denuò re-
uocarentur? Neque verò alicubi consuetum est, neque ratione vlla
ferendum videtur, vt alienigenæ in earum rerum vsu, quæ regno-
rum sunt propriæ, Indigenis præferantur: quin potiùs singularis
beneficii loco ducitur, si pares fiant: id quod nos Ciuitatibus Impe-
rii si quæ petiuissent, iamdudum ob singulare Amicitiæ nostræ studi-
um, benignè concedere statueramus.

Inte-

*Interim verò quibuscunque Imperij subditis, in Dominijs no-
stris liberè versandi . & more exterorum negotiandi faculta-
tem nunquam negauimus. Domum propriam in Metropoli nostra,
vbi suis moribus viuerent, ex gratia illis semper permisimus: ita
quidem, vt Iure conqueri non possint, se vti denunciatos hostes apud
nos habitos vnquam fuisse. Quod verò de damnis acceptis inferunt,
ita se habet. Cum superioribus hisce annis bello Hispanico implica-
ri cœpissemus, more aliorum Principum, bellica presidia hostibus in-
tercludenda, quantum in nobis fuerat decreuimus: eaq́; de re Vici-
nas Ciuitates præmonuimus: atque si qui inhibita hoc bello tempore in Hispaniam transportare niterentur, eosdem veluti auxiliato-
res atque hostium complices, aliqua ex parte habendos, atque inhi-
bitorum confiscatione multandos declarauimus: his actis Classia-
rij nostri in plurimas Hanseaticorum Naues rebus inhibitis onu-
stas inciderunt: Nauibus verò ac Nautis ex indulgentia dimissis,
bona tantum inhibita Iure belli ac Regni nostri institutis fisco com-
miserunt. Quæ quidem illorum Damna; (de alijs enim nihil nobis
constat) multa nomine Iure optimo illata nullo æquitatis colore
restituenda veniunt.*

*Monopolium porrò, de quo Hanseatici subditos nostros crimin-
antur, calumniæ potius quàm veræ accusationis rationem præ se
ferre videtur: ab ipsis enim Imperij subditis, qui Londini resident,
diligenter inquiri iussimus, si quid solidi de iniquis subditorum nostrorum negotiandi rationibus referre possent, illi verò ingenuè re-
sponderunt se nihil ea de re in commissis habere: acturos tamen se
quamprimum per literas cum suis maioribus. Cumq́; demùm quid
responsi acciperint, id totum fideliter relaturos. Questionem præterea ea de re cũ subditis nostris institui mandauimus: illi verò authenticis scriptis edocent, negotiandi ipsorum rationes à plurimis
ciuitatibus in Belgio, Prussia, atque alibi vti honestissimas probari.
Atque cùm duæ Imperij Ciuitates sint, quæ cum nostris maximè
negotiantur, Lubeca & Hamburgum, illarum altera publicis literis (vt nostri ostendunt) testata est, ipsorum negotiationem ab omni
Monopoly suspicione vacuam esse, seq́; illius obiectæ criminationis
participem nũquam fuisse: Vbi verò Hanseaticorum Institores, plura ea de re ex Dominorum suorum expectata comissione, in scriptis opposuerint, se quæque pluribus in scriptis responsuros humiliter
obtulerunt.*

*obtulerunt.*

*Ad Augustanum deniqꝫ de comercijs inhibendis mandatum quod attinet, non satis intelligimus, qua ratione Imperij Principes recte informati, de priuilegijs aut alijs quibuscunque ad Iura Regni nostri, ab imperij Legibus semper absoluti, pertinentibus, cognitionem suscipere potuerint: neque sanè videmus quibus documentis eam in sententiam adduci possent, vt commerciorum inhibitionem Imperio, Serenitati vestræ, sibi ipsis, aut Imperij Ciuitatibus, vtilem fore arbitrarentur. Quamobrem Mandatum illud vti obreptitiè impetratum, Iure optimo hactenus suspensum fuisse, ac deinceps suspendendum esse meritò existimamus. Interim verò ne quid mutuæ amicitiæ nostræ desit, Imperij subditos qui in Dominijs nostris fortè versabuntur, more solito benigna protectione nostra clementer tuebimur: atque si Lubeca, Hamburgium, aut alia Serenitatis vestræ Ciuitas, ipsius nomine gratiam à nobis submissè postulauerint, quæ negotiandi rationes maiori ipsorum commodo instituendas cupiant, Serenitatis vestræ commendationem plurimum apud nos momenti habuisse facilé intelligent: nos vicissim amanter petimus, vt parẽ gratiam subditis nostris in ipsius Dominijs clementer impertire Serenitas vestra non grauetur. Eidemꝗ interim fœlicia omnia à DEO Optimo Maximo precamur. Datæ è Regia nostra Richemundana, octauo Nouembris, Anno Domini 1595, Regni verò nostri xxxvij.*

Serénitatis veſtræ Soror & Conſanguinea

ELIZABETHA.

# Attestation of the citie of Antwerp,

## on the Companie of the Merchants Aduenturers behalfe.

Niuerfis & fingulis noftras præfentes literas teftimoniales vifuris vel audituris, Burgimagiftri & Scabini Ciuitatis Antuerpienfis in Ducatu Brabantiæ falutem. Cùm pium fit, ac rationi confanum Veritati teftimonium perhibere, præfertim fi pro conferuando alterius Iure requiramur. Hinc eft quod obnixè rogati ex parte Magnificorum Dominorum Gubernatoris, Affiftentium, & communium Mercatorum nationis Anglica, præfentibus hifce fidem facimus, & atteftamur dictos Mercatores nationis Anglica, qui pluribus abhinc annis in hac noftra Ciuitate Antuerpienfi refiderunt & adhuc refident, honeftam, lucitam, & Reipub. vtilem femper exercuiffe negotiationem, & etiamnum adhuc exercere in emendis, vendendis, & permutandis mercimonijs alijfq, legitimis contractibus ineundis, neque vllum feciffe difcrimen inter Mercatores cum quibus contraherent cuius illi effent nationis, dummodo foluendo & fpectatæ fidei forent, quibus interdum præfente, interdum ad tempus credita pecunia Pannos, Carfeas, aliáfq, merces fuas promifcuè femper vendidère, & adhuc vendunt. In quorum fidem hafce literas figillo huius Ciuitatis ad caufas muniri fecimus. Datum die 19. menfis Aprilis, Anno Domini 1582.

## Attestation of 28. Merchants in Antwerp of fundry Nations, concerning the Companies orderly Trade and cleareneffe from Monopoly.

Niuerfis & fingulis præfentes literas, infpecturis fiue audituris, Burgimagiftri, Scabini, & Confules Ciuitatis Antuerpiæ falutem, Notum facimus ac harum ferie teftamur, Quòd die infra fcripto ad inftantiam magnificorum Dominorum Gubernatoris, Affiftentium, & communium

Merca-

*Mercatorũ nationis Anglica in hac ciuitate residẽtiũ coram nobis*
*comparuerunt D.D. Ludouicus Guicciardini Floretinus, Carolus*
*Lam Franchi, Ioan. Angelus Vergano, Gasper Reuelasco, Lam-*
*bertus Läberti, Simon Tassa, Bartholomæus Luquini, Bartholo-*
*mæus Balbi, natione Itali, Domini Iacobus de Pardo, Petrus dala*
*Pena Hispani, Domini Ferdinandus Ximenes, Rodrigo de Vega,*
*Ludouicus Ferdinandes, Simon Rodrigues Portugallenses siue Lu-*
*sitani, D.D. Ioannes Putz, Iacobus Lange, Ieremias Gennis Ger-*
*mani, Domini Theodoricus de Moy, Ludouicus de Becque, Iaco-*
*bus van Yeweruen, Gualterus Schot, Henricus Moons, Daniel de*
*Lommel, Arnoldus Boudewijns, Nicolaus Rampart, Henricus van*
*Homssen, Ioannes vanden Steene, & Iacobus Schot, Ciues & inco-*
*li huius Opidi, omnesq̃, Mercatores, Bursam eiusdem Oppidi fre-*
*quentantes, Viri fide digni, nobisq̃ probè cogniti, Qui medijs illo-*
*rum iuramentis solemniter præstitis iurauerunt & affirmauerunt*
*primo ad id iuridice citati prædictos Mercatores Nationis Angli-*
*cæ, tam in hac Ciuitate Antuerpia, quàm alijs locis vbi negotian-*
*tur, Iustam, licitamq̃ negotiationem exercuisse, & adhuc exerce-*
*re, neque quantum rescire potuerunt eosdem Mercatores profes-*
*sionem fecisse fœnerandi vel dandi pecunias ad vsuram aut Mono-*
*polijs vsos fuisse, verúm è contrario eosdem semper exercuisse &*
*in ijs exercere iustam negotiationem, consistentem in emẽdis, ven-*
*dendis, & permutandis mercibus alijsque legitimis Contractibus*
*ineundis. Itemq̃ præfatos Mercatores Anglicos illorum Pannos,*
*Carseas, aliasq̃ merces omnibus & quibuscunque Nationibus*
*Christiani Orbis sine discrimine vendere, prout etiam dicti Depo-*
*nentes nunquam rescire potuerunt, quod dicti Mercatores inter se*
*aliquas erexerint Ordinationes aut Statuta, quibus suis Pannis,*
*Cariseis, aut alijs mercibus certum præfigant prætium, quo & non*
*minoris diuendi debeant, Quinimo ipsorum negotiationem semper*
*fuisse & esse liberam. Pretereà Mercatores Anglicos in hac Ci-*
*uitate Antuerpiensi & Embdæ, aut alibi locorum residentes pro*
*magna parte diuersos habere Ministros & Institores, & separata*
*Domicilia & Magazena, vt plurimum seorsum & separatim ne-*
*gotiando pro lubito alij ad tempus credita pecunia, itemque alij*
*maiori, alij minori pratio, vel etiam commutatione mercium & a-*
*lias, sine dolo malo, In cuius rei testimonium, sigillum ad causas*

Q
*huius*

*huius Ciuitatis Antuerpiæ præsentibus apponi fecimus, Die decima nona mensis Aprilis, Anno Domini Millesimo quingentesimo octuagesimo secundo.*

## Attestation of the Towne of Embden in East-Friseland, on the behalfe of the Companie of Merchants Aduenturers.

VNiuersis & singulis cuiuscunque Ordinis, & Dignitatis has nostras literas visuris, siue cognituris N s Consules, Senatores, atque Magistratus vrbis Embdæ sitæ in Frisiæ Orientali sub tutela sacræ Cæsareæ Maiestatis, Domini nostri clementissimi, & sacri Romani Imperij existente Comitatu post debitam, & demissam salutis, atque obseruantiæ nostræ significationem, notum publice facimus, ac testamur: Quum Ornatissima Anglica natio aliquot annos in hac Ciuitate commorata varij generis mercimonia exerceant, & per suum Secretarium, ac Procuratorem doctum, & ornatum virum Dominum Ioannem Moer, à nobis in pleno Senatu testimonium de ratione Negotiationis, & mercatus sui petierint, minimè id quidem officij, quantum nobis constat, eis recusandum putauimus: Quamobrem pro certo affirmamus, ac testamur publicè, quòd dicta Anglicæ Nationis Mercatores, eorumq; ministri, & negotiorum gestores (quos Aduenturarios vocant) quatenus nobis cognitū est, quàm diu apud nos fuerunt, sese semper honestè, & legitimè in suis Contractibus, & Negotiationibus gessisse, & adhuc gerere honestum, liberum, ac licitum mercatum in Pannis, Cariseijs, aliisq; mercimonijs emēdis, vendēdis & permutandis exercere atque tractare, neque aliter agere, quàm probos, & idoneos Mercatores, & Negotiatores, agere par est, & decet. Proinde quum Magistratus officij sit ad id requisiti, veritati ferre testimonium, nostram quoque mentem ea de republicè profitendam censuimus. In cuius rei confirmationem sigillum nostrum ad causas scienter appendimus: Anno Domini supra sesqui millesimum Octuagesimo secundo, vigesimo octauo die Iulij.

Atte-

## Attestation of foureteene Merchants in Stade of sundry places, on the behalfe of the Companie of Merchants Aduenturers.

VNIVERSIS ET SINGULIS præsentes has literas visuris vel audituris, quocunque dignitatis, honoris, & eminentiæ gradu fuerint, Nos CONSVLES & Senatores Reipub. STADENSIS, Archiepiscopatus Bremensis, post debitam officiorum nostrorum oblationem & honorificam salutationem notum facimus publicéq, attestamur, quod ad instantiam Magnifici spectabilium & discretorum Domini Thomæ Ferrers, Regiæ Maiestatis Anglicæ Agentis, & hactenus apud nos Præfecti aliorumq, Assistentium & Mercatorum Anglicorum Adventurariæ Societatis, per aliquot annos in nostra Ciuitate residentium, & iam tandem abitum fauente Neptuno, dudum sperantium, coram Nobis cumparuerunt legitimè iudicialitérque citati spectabiles & honesti viri, fidéq, digni testes & Bursam Forumq, nostræ Ciuitatis quotidiè frequentantes, Domini Iohannes Calandrinus Lucensis Italus, Bartolomæus Pels, Wilhelmus Bartolotti, Iacobus de Greve, Antonius Boots, Hieronymus Hester, Simon de Beck, Matthias de Kestelt, Antuerpienses, Franciscus Boudewin Buscoducensis, Wilhelmus de Bari, Dornacensis, Antonius Engelbrecht, Aquisgranesis, Antonius Geir, Coloniensis, Ioan. Philippus Stamler, & Georgius Mauritius, Augustani, satisq, & sufficieter de veritate dicenda admoniti, stipulato, sub fide datæru dextrarũ, in vim & ad effectum corporalis iuramenti, quod se desuper re ipsa præstare, si requirantur, non gravari affirmabant, deposuerunt & attestati sunt, sibi quam notissimum seq̃ ipsos expertos esse, Adventurarios mercatores Anglicæ nationis, huc vsque in nostra Ciuitate residentes, & iam ad abitum paratos, non Pannos modò, Cariseias, Baiettas, sed & alias varias & diuersas merces ex Anglia huc advectas, quibuscunque orbis Christiani incolis, absque ullo discrimine Nationis aut Religionis, vendere & vicissim qualiacunque bona, sibi placentia, ab aliis redimere aut in solutũ accipere atque hinc in Angliam remittere solere, itemq,

omni-

omnibus omninò Mercatoribus similiter liberum esse, suas merces
in Angliam deportari, ibíq́; vendi, aliásque quascunque dènuò
emi & in Germaniam atque alias quascunque regiones soluto solito telonio transuehi procurare, atque hanc Anglos Aduenturarios Mercatores legitimam iustámque negotiationem in emendo
& vendendo aliísq́; licitis contractibus ineundis non minus atque
alios quoslibet negotiatores in nostra Ciuitate hactenus exercuisse,
nec sibi notum esse, aut se vnquam audiuisse, quod Angli Mercatores hactenus apud nos residentes, professionem fœnerandi pecuni-
ásûe ad vsuram dandæ fecerint, multò minus pacta aut statuta inter
se constituerint, quibus se inuicem obstrinxerint, aut suas merces
certo precio, quod citra pœnam mutare nefas esset, vendendas aut
alienas similiter emendas: sed è contrà, omnibus esse cognitum, eiusdem bonitatis, signíque Pannos, Cariseias, Baiettas, aliáque quæ-
cunque mercimonia apud plurimos Anglos Aduenturariæ Societatis Mercatores, in diuersis Tabernis & domiciliis separatis exi-
stentes, tam Dominos quàm Factores, aut famulos siue institores,
vno & eodem temporis momento reperiri, eáq́; non vno, sed diuersissimo pretio, ad duas, tres, quatuor, quinque, & plures etiã libras,
& si nunc maiore, nunc etiam minore pretio, præsente, vel ad tempus credita pecunia, datis obligationibus, vel facta mercium permutatione, pro vt cuiusque res tulerit, emi, atque pariter alias
merces diuersimodo illis vendi posse, nec vnquam ad notitiam suam
peruenisse aut se rescire potuisse Anglos Aduenturariæ Societatis
Negotiatores, quousque hic Stadæ vixissent, de Monopolio iure
& legitimè accusatos, multò minus vnquam à quoquam conuictos
fuisse. Absque omni dolo, malo, fraude, & sinistra machinatione.
In cuius rei testimonium præsentibus solitum nostra Ciuitatis Se-
cretum appendi scienter iussimus. Data a.d. 11x. Mensis Fe-
bruarii, Anno salutifera natiuitatis vnici Domini & Redempto-
ris nostri IESV CHRISTI, millesimo quingentesimo nona-
gesimo octauo.

Attesta-

# Atteſtation of the Towne of Midelburgh in Zeland, on the behalfe of the Companie of M. M. Aduenturers.

Niuerſis & ſingulis noſtras præſentes literas teſtimoniales viſuris vel audituris, Burgimagiſtri, Scabini, Senatoreſ́q́, Ciuitatis Middelburgenſis in Comitatu Zelandiæ Sálutem: Quum pium ſit, & rationi conſonum veritati teſtimonium perhibere, præſertim ſi pro conſeruando alterius Iure requiratur, hinc eſt quòd obnixè rogati ex parte magnificorum Dominorum Gubernatoris, Aſſiſtentium, & commúnium Mercatorum Nationis Angliæ, & Aduenturariæ Societatis præſentibus hiſce fidem facimus, & atteſtamur, dictos Mercatores Nationis Angliæ, qui pluribus abhinc annis in hac noſtra Ciuitate Middelburgenſi reſiderunt, & adhuc reſident, honeſtam, licitam, & Reipublicæ vtilem ſemper exercuiſſe Negotiationem, & adhuc etiamnum exercere in emendis, vendendis, & permutandis mercibus, aliiſ́q́ legitimis contractibus ineundis, neque vllum feciſſe diſcrimen inter Mercatores, quibuſcum contraherent, cuiuſcunque eſſent Nationis, dúmodo forent ſoluendo, & ſpectatæ fidei, quibus interdum præſenti, interdum credita pecuniâ Pannos, Cariſeias, aliaſ́q́, merces ſuas promiſcuè ſemper vendidère, & adhuc vendunt : Atteſtamur præterea nunquam nobis notum fuiſſe, aut audiuiſſe vnquam, quòd dicti Angli Mercatores Aduenturarii hactenus apud nos reſidentes profeſſionem fœnerandi, pecuniáſque ad vſuram dandi fecerint, multò minus pacta, aut ſtatuta inter ſe conſtituerint, quibus ſe inuicem obſtrinxerint, aut ſuas merces certo pretio, quòd vltra pœnam mutare nefas eſſet, vel aliter vendendas, aut alienas ſimiliter emendas, ſed è contrà, omnibus eſſe cognitum, eiuſdem bonitatis ſigniſ́q́, Pannos, Cariſeias, aliaſ́q́, quæcunqne mercimonia apud plurimos Anglos prædictæ Societatis Mercatores, in diuerſis tabernis, & domiciliis ſeparatis exiſtentes, tàm Dominos, quàm Factores, aut Famulos, ſiue Inſtitores vno & eodem temporis momẽto

Q 3                    reperiri,

reperiri, eaq́ non vno, sed diuersissimo prætio ad duas, tres, quatu-
or, quinque, & plures libras, & sic nunc maiori, nunc minori prætio, præsenti, vel ad tempus credita pecunia, datis obligationibus,
vel facta mercium permutatione, prout cuiusque res tulerit, emi,
atq; pariter alias merces diuersimodo illis vendi posse: Nec vnquam ad notitiam nostram peruenisse, aut nos rescire potuisse,
Anglos Aduenturariæ Societatis prædicta Negotiatores, quousque hic Middelburgi vixerunt, de Monopolio Iure, & legitimè accusatos, multò minus vnquam à quopiam cõuictos fuisse, abs-
què omni dolo malo, fraude, & sinistra machinatione. In cuius rei
testimonium alterius Secretatiorum nostrorum manu Instru-
mentum hoc subsignari, nec non sigillum ad causas apponere iussimus, vt in simili negotio apud nos est consuetum: Actum septimo
die mensis Iulii Anno Domini Millesimo Sexcentesimo.

## Schotte.

## F I N I S.